A PARENT'S GUIDE TO VIRTUAL LEARNING

A PARENT'S GUIDE TO VIRTUAL LEARNING

How to Help Your Child Thrive in an Online Classroom

Dr. Felicia Durden

ULYSSES PRESS

Published in the US by:
Ulysses Press
PO Box 3440
Berkeley, CA 94703
www.ulyssespress.com

ISBN: 978-1-64604-184-8
Library of Congress Control Number: 2021931496

Printed in Canada by Marquis Book Printing
10 9 8 7 6 5 4 3 2 1

Acquisitions editor: Ashten Evans
Managing editor: Claire Chun
Editor: Scott Calamar
Proofreader: Renee Rutledge
Front cover design: Olivia Croom Hammerman
Cover art: © Shirstok/shutterstock.com; computer © RaiDztor/shutterstock.com
Interior design: what!design @ whatweb.com
Interior art: shutterstock.com—page 12 © Lyudmyla Kharlamova; page 21 © Mallmo (left), © All About Space (top right), © Photographee (bottom right); page 64 © Maxim Cherednichenko; page 65 © Flashon Studio; page 94 © Brian A Jackson; page 99 © Duda Vasiliir; page 105 © Lorelyn Medina; page 111 © mickallnice; page 116 © Nadya Art; page 117 © mattasbestos; page 122 © Dzm1try

This book is dedicated to the memory of my parents, Virgil and Nevida Jack, who instilled a love for learning and reading in me at a very young age. You will never be forgotten.

CONTENTS

CHAPTER 8
STRATEGIES FOR READING 81

CHAPTER 9
STRATEGIES FOR WRITING 103

CHAPTER 10
HOW TO STAY UPBEAT AND NOT
LOSE IT 133

INTRODUCTION

"I think I can. I think I can. I think I can. I think I can. I thought I could. I thought I could..."
—The Little Engine That Could

I have received countless requests from parents about how to support their children with online learning. As a mother, school administrator, aunt, and sister, my family members, as well as the community, have asked me for any ideas or strategies that they can use to help them get through virtual learning without losing it.

With the onset of COVID-19, we were all thrown off-kilter when schools around the world had to shutter and parents were asked to play a primary role in the education of their children in ways that they have never been expected to perform.

Our vocabulary now includes words like "Zoom," "Google Meet," "Clever Badges," and "Reboot," to name a few, and we are all feeling technology fatigue from being in front of a computer screen hours upon hours each day.

You may be thinking, "I don't have a degree in teaching" and "I don't know where to start to support my child. I am barely hanging on, trying to keep them from running away from the computer screen each day. I need help!"

Well, help is here. *A Parent's Guide to Virtual Learning* is a crash course in virtual education. The tips and tools in this book will boot you up so you can support your child with confidence.

This book is written as a resource to provide parents with tips, tricks, and tools you can immediately put into play to help ensure that your child has a successful online learning experience. This book, however, is twofold: it is also written as a support for parents all over the world to enable you to practice self-care and increase awareness so you can be your best you to support your child adequately.

Each chapter includes tips that you can put into place immediately to start supporting your child so they get the most out of this new method of learning. Topics covered include talking to your child's teacher, setting boundaries, troubleshooting technical issues, helping your child solve math problems, and the list goes on and on. We cover the big issues, but most importantly, we include strategies for the smaller issues that without a proper response can become huge ones.

But You're Not a Teacher

I was a K–12 teacher, reading specialist, and district administrator for over fifteen years. I currently work as an elementary school principal, and I know that the challenge of supporting your children with online learning is daunting. But, as a parent myself, I also know that you can do this.

I know the struggles you face—I know that you're not only dealing with your own professional and emotional work, but also that teaching itself may seem confusing. Many parents have noted that teaching has changed in the past few years, and the way kids today learn math for example, is not the way we learned when we were in school.

Yes, the methods of instruction have changed a lot in the past decade, and now, the addition of online education to the mix can seem overwhelming. I want you to take a deep breath and realize that we are all in the same boat. The COVID-19 pandemic has affected the education of students across the globe. What I want to offer in this book is a refuge with easy-to-implement tips that will make your life and your child's life easier.

What You'll Find in This Book

Here is a quick rundown on the chapters in the book.

In the first chapter, I will cover the different types of virtual learning environments and how they work. This first chapter lays a foundation on how virtual learning has expanded and grown, and what that means for you and your child.

Chapter Two is all about setting up a learning environment in your home, including organizing an optimal space for educating your child.

In Chapter Three, I provide you with the strategies you need to establish a routine that will help you start each day with confidence and focus.

Setting clear boundaries and sticking with them will be explored in Chapter Four. The home-school connection and communicating with your child's teacher is the focus of Chapter Five.

Chapter Six will provide you with tips on how to handle the inevitable technical issues that you will face.

Chapters Seven, Eight, and Nine will provide you with techniques on how to best support your child with their math, reading, and writing. These chapters are filled with best practices and secrets that teachers use to engage their students and help them learn. You will get a crash course in online teaching pedagogy.

Ensuring you practice self-care is the focus of Chapter Ten. The final two chapters will include final thoughts and a chapter filled with online resources and tools you can use at home with your child.

Before you dive in, I do want to note that this book is outlined in a way to enable you to quickly go to the chapters and find the specific support you're looking for. Don't feel the need to read every single page if you require a specific type of information. For instance, if you find your child is struggling with a math concept, you can quickly turn to Chapter Seven and find ideas on easy things you can do at home to address their mathematics challenge.

Children Can Learn at High Levels in the Virtual Learning Space

As a public school educator and administrator with over twenty years of experience under my belt, I can attest that children *can* learn at high levels in the online environment. According to research, this occurs when we provide students with adequate support and intervention as soon as we see the need arise. This book is full of ideas on how to do just that as your child is learning virtually. I know that many parents are afraid that their children will digress in their learning while working online. Please rest assured that the information in this book will help you alleviate this worry by familiarizing you with virtual learning. You'll get to know the ins and outs of the different virtual learning models so you are prepared to assist your child. With proper support at home, parents can play a pivotal role in helping their children succeed in the virtual learning space.

Now let's get going!

In the upcoming chapters we will work on developing an understanding on how virtual learning evolved and how you can use proven methods to help your child as they are learning virtually.

CHAPTER 1

WHAT IS VIRTUAL LEARNING?

"Alone we can do so little; together we can do so much."

—Helen Keller

We Are in This Together

Many of us were taken by surprise when our children were required to learn virtually in the spring of 2020. The coronavirus pandemic affected the lives of millions upon millions of parents across the globe. Within a matter of weeks, an uncountable number of children around the world were beginning to learn in some sort of virtual learning environment.

This has come as a huge shift in how we are educating our students, and it has put a lot of stress on families around the world. The biggest stressor is on what to do to help children learn from home and maintain balance and harmony in the home.

One thing is for sure—as a human race we are wired to come together in times of need. Ideas like rallying the troops and pulling up our bootstraps come to mind when thinking about all the innovative ways parents are reaching out to get support for their children's education.

I have been impressed with the resiliency I have seen in parents all around the world. New things like parent pods and school study groups have popped up to provide moral support, offer a lending hand, and serve as a way of connecting as we all work to find solutions to make the virtual learning space effective for our families.

> **Success Tip:** Parent pods are learning support groups that parents use to have their children work with other students either virtually or in person on academics. The goal of learning pods is to bring in some socialization for students and help for parents. The pods are popping up all around. The best way to find one is to search for "learning pods" or "pandemic pods" in your area.

The fact is—virtual learning can be challenging. I know that the struggle is real with keeping your kids on task as they learn, while you possibly hold down your full-time job or care for other children or adults that are in the home. In this chapter, we will explore the history of virtual learning and set the stage for ways you can ensure you understand the model that is used by your child so you can ask the right questions and provide the optimal support.

Virtual Learning Defined

First, let's examine what virtual learning is. "Virtual learning" refers to teaching that occurs online or by using methods other than placing students in a school-room with a teacher. There are now more than one thousand virtual academies in the United States. Virtual academies are schools that educate students virtu-ally 100 percent of the time, offering only online learning options. This differs from schools that use virtual learning as part of their teaching methodology. Virtual academies are made up of different grade-level configurations. I have seen elementary virtual academies and high school academies. Virtual learning, employing the use of computers, gained popularity in the 1980s, mainly on college campuses, when online degrees became a good option for working adults. These students needed a program that was flexible, allowing them to work full time while going to school. Virtual learning also combats another barrier: location. It allows students to go to school in a state other than where they reside. Virtual learning literally opened up the world for students who were seeking to advance their education.

The Beginning of Virtual Learning

Virtual learning is not new. In fact, in a more traditional form, it has been around since the 1940s. Have you heard of correspondence courses? I remember taking a correspondence course on drawing when I was a young girl. I found out about it in one of my mother's magazines, and I completed work that was sent to me and mailed it back to the company. I remember being so proud of my certificate of completion. In fact, I still have that certificate in my memory book.

This type of distance learning is still happening today! Some schools are using packets that are mailed out or are picked up from school so kids can work on them. The packets are then returned to school and graded. This method is most frequently used with primary-age students to work on handwriting, reading, and sometimes other subjects.

We have become a lot more sophisticated in our methods than when I took my correspondence course. Today, we are able to more clearly identify students' needs and give them work that is differentiated, meaning based on their individual requirements.

The Modern Development of Virtual Learning

Schools began to pick up on this trend in the late '80s. With computers and the internet being more accessible, more options were provided for students to take their classes virtually instead of coming into the brick-and-mortar classroom. Many families found this to be a good option if they lived in remote areas, had children who experienced difficulty with face-to-face learning, or were interested in trying something innovative. The first online models were mainly used at the high school level, but we soon saw virtual academies, or online schools opening that supported students at middle and elementary levels.

By the late '80s and early '90s, full online learning began to evolve. We started to see more online learning platforms developing and schools beginning to embrace students taking their courses solely online. In a full online learning model, the student does all of their assignments electronically, and their only interaction with their teacher is via technology.

Full online institutions, such as the University of Phoenix, as well as a plethora of other institutes of higher education, including Capella University and Walden University, which offered working adults the opportunity to further their education from home, demonstrated that the model could be effective. Elementary and secondary schools began offering distance or virtual learning for their students.

That's our history lesson on virtual learning. Now let's take a look at the different models and the tools you can use to support your child, depending on the virtual learning space you are currently working in.

Virtual Learning Models

You will find different models of virtual learning, depending on which one(s) your child's school or district has adopted.

The three main types include the full online model, the hybrid, or staggered model, and the distance-learning model.

- The full online model is where kids are online for their entire learning day. Full online learning involves students completing all their lessons using technology with the support of a teacher. In a full online learning model, the student does all of their assignments electronically, and their only interaction with their teacher is through the computer. I would say from my observation that this is the most popular model currently being used across the nation. Full online learning can also be one of the most stressful models, according to parents.

- The hybrid, sometimes called staggered model, is where students attend some of their classes in person and some online There is also a hybrid model where kids check in with their teacher online in the morning and work independently for the rest of the day.

  In this book, we will cover the most popular hybrid model, in which students attend a physical classroom a few days a week and then participate online the remaining days. In the model, the student has the ability to interact with their teacher in person and is instructed on what to do during the online time. Many schools keep the days consistent so parents do not have a hard time figuring out the schedule. This may mean that your child goes to school in person two days per week and works online three days per week or vice versa.

- Finally, there is a distance-learning model, where students are physically given packets to work on at home, and teachers check in with the students after they turn those in, then give feedback. This is similar to the correspondence courses we talked about earlier. Some of these schools require parents to pick up their packets and drop them off when they are finished. Some mail them out and have the kids return them by mail. Others offer them as supports to supplement the learning, but they are not required. Again, these are the main ways I have seen learning packets used, but I am sure there are some other creative ways that schools are using learning packets.

These are not the only virtual learning models out there, but they are currently the most popular ones.

In some districts, students move in and out of different models depending on the current needs of the school, district, and state of events. Regardless of which model your child follows, we'll help you successfully maneuver this new world in a stress-free manner.

Parent Tips for Virtual Learning Support

Following are tips for the main virtual learning models I have seen used consistently. Again, these are not the only online models out there. Schools have some pretty creative ways to meet their students' needs, but these are the scenarios that you are most likely to encounter.

Distance Learning

If your child's school is using learning packets, here are some tips for you. Make sure that you understand what the teacher expects students to complete and what they want turned in. For example, let's say you are told that your child is expected to read for thirty minutes each day. You should ask what evidence the teacher wants to prove that they have done their reading.

If your child is using packets, make sure that they read the directions carefully or that you read them to make sure work is completed correctly. I don't know how many times I've seen students complete a worksheet without reading the directions, and they circle all the words that rhyme with the wrong sound, for instance.

Another tip is to help your kids pace themselves if the packets are to be done over the course of a week. Set a time each day for your child to work on the packet and give them benchmark goals to accomplish each day. For example, if your child has a twenty-page packet, advise them to break it up and complete four pages each day. You don't want your child rushing through all the work at the end of the week right before the due date. That will be stressful for both you and your child.

If your child cannot complete the work because it's too difficult for them, immediately reach out to the teacher and find out what your options are. Often teachers have alternative work packets, or possibly you can schedule some time for the teacher to talk with your child to provide guidance and tutoring.

FOUR-STEP PLAN FOR PACKET COMPLETION

STEP 1: Look over the packet work.

STEP 2: Ensure your child understands the directions to complete each packet page.

STEP 3: Reach out to your child's teacher immediately if you do not understand something or your child struggles with any of the concepts in the packet work.

STEP 4: Create a schedule for packet completion. Pace yourself so that you are not left with fifteen pages to complete in one day.

Full Online Learning

When you're working with a full online model, the first step is to make sure you test your computers and the programs that your child is asked to use. This can be one of the most frustrating things about being fully online: Your child is expected to log in at a certain time of the morning and your sign-in does not work. Does this sound familiar? Be on top of what the expectations are for logging in, and you have accomplished half the battle of full online learning. This may sound like a simple tip, but believe me, a nonworking password can send you into a tailspin that can become an overwhelming burden over time.

As with the learning packets, if your child is learning exclusively online, be sure to get a clear understanding of what is required to be completed each day. Some students will have exercises that they must finish independently after their teacher provides instruction. Many parents have noted that their kids had assignments to complete, but they were not aware of this until report cards came out and their child was marked down for not completing their work.

If you don't remember anything else in this chapter, please remember to check in with your child's teacher to ensure you are clear on what the expectations are. Many issues can be avoided simply by asking for clarification.

Seek clarification!

The great thing about full virtual learning is that you can often get online with the teacher during instructional time to ask questions. Most schools will also have virtual office hours that you and your child can use to meet with the teacher if you are experiencing any issues.

TIPS FOR FULL ONLINE LEARNING

TIP 1: Make sure you can log in. (Does your internet need updating? Secure a faster internet connection or upgrade your internet equipment if necessary.)

TIP 2: Make sure you can get into all learning platforms and applications.

TIP 3: Seek clarification! Ensure you understand what the expectation is in the virtual learning classroom.

TIP 4: Use virtual office hours to meet with your child's teacher if you have questions.

Hybrid Models

The nice thing about this model is that on the days your child is in school, they can get support and questions answered about areas that they may be struggling with. The downside is that students can have a hard time being home and working online after being in the classroom with their teacher and peers the day before. In this section, I will provide some ideas on how to make the days you work together at home seamless.

In the hybrid model, you will use the same online learning support tips that are listed above for the days/times your child is working from home.

To seamlessly transition your child from being at school to working online at home is to set defined boundaries and clearly explain to your child that the same expectations apply whether they work at school or at home. Many children find it hard to grasp schooling at home while in the home setting. Home is home, so they might begin to exhibit behavior that is not "school-like" in the house. Nip this in the bud immediately by stating clearly to your child in terms that they can understand that on the days they work from home, they are still in school. This one tip will save you from so many power struggles between you and your child when it comes to understanding the expectations. It again is a simple thing to do that will yield a huge harvest. Below are the steps to follow to explain and set the expectations with your child:

TIPS FOR HYBRID LEARNING

STEP 1: Find a place in your home that is quiet and free from distraction.

STEP 2: Sit with your child, ensuring you have eye contact with them.

STEP 3: Explain to your child that they will be going to school in person X number of days a week and working from home online X number of days. (Give them the exact days and times so they can be clear on what to expect.)

STEP 4: Explain that the days they work from home are still school days, just like the days when they attend classes in person. (This step is pivotal because kids often find being home a relaxing retreat and a place where they have fun and no pressure to do schoolwork.)

STEP 5: Assure your child that you will be there to support them.

STEP 6: Take time to answer any questions your child may have.

VIRTUAL LEARNING MODELS

DISTANCE	Students complete work packets at home, which are mailed or dropped off at school.
FULL ONLINE	Students complete all of their learning online.
HYBRID	Students sometimes attend in person and complete online work.

Closing Thoughts on Virtual Learning

The first thing I am going to ask you to do before going any further in this book is to give yourself some grace. We live in a world of comparison. Facebook, Instagram, and Pinterest don't make life easy. Don't buy into the perfection monster, but know that you are doing your best each and every day, and by reading this book and those like it, you are taking phenomenal steps to help make virtual learning a positive experience for your family. I want to congratulate you for the care and effort you are putting into your child's education. Don't worry, don't compare, and don't buy into perfection. Give yourself some grace, and let's do this!

CHAPTER 2

PREPARING FOR VIRTUAL LEARNING

"An ounce of prevention is worth a pound of cure."

—Benjamin Franklin

In order to be ready for virtual learning, there are a few initial steps you will need to take to assure a pleasant online experience for both yourself and your child. We will begin by assessing your current situation so that you are not taken by surprise and are, most importantly, prepared for the benefits of virtual learning.

Enough cannot be said about the significance of proper preparation. As an experienced educator, I can attest to the value of having all your ducks in a row when it comes to setting up a proper learning environment. The environment that you will create for your child should be the number one priority, as we know that having an organized workspace helps children learn at higher levels. An organized workspace also helps to decrease stress and anxiety, which can be another deterrent to a positive home-learning experience.

In this chapter, we will discuss ways to make your home school friendly, and we will give you suggested tools and materials that will make learning from home fun, engaging, and effective.

Why Does Learning Environment Matter?

The environment where we work has a strong correlation to our productivity. If the learning environment is cluttered and distracting, learning levels diminish. Think about a time when you were learning something new. You had to pay close attention to the instructions that were being given, and you had to process the information in your brain and make sense of it so you could understand and execute it. Your child is learning new information on a daily basis. If the workspace is distracting and unorganized, some of their attention will be taken off the task of learning.

Teachers spend hours upon hours thinking about setting up their classrooms in a way that is functional and makes the best use of the space. In this section, we will provide some ideas for creating a learning space for your child that will optimize their learning but not overwhelm you.

In my first year as a teacher, I took over for another teacher midyear. I literally started the day following my interview. This meant I had no time to organize my classroom and set up my learning environment. Let's just say my first week was not a bowl of cherries. I immediately regrouped and came in over the weekend to organize and set up my classroom. When the students returned on Monday, they were met with a clean and organized space. Their behaviors almost immediately changed as they felt less stress and anxiety because of the order they now had in their learning environment.

Assessing Your Environment

We want to start by having you assess your current home situation. Please take the time to complete the survey below. Using the data from this survey will help you determine where you need to spend time to set up the most viable learning environment for your child.

AT-HOME LEARNING ENVIRONMENT SURVEY

I have a space set up where my child can work.	■ YES ■ NO
My child's workspace has pens and pencils readily available.	■ YES ■ NO
The background behind my child has no distractions.	■ YES ■ NO
The area where my child is working is free of clutter.	■ YES ■ NO

How did you do on the survey? Remember, this is just to get you thinking about your current situation so we can work on transforming your child's designated workspace into a viable learning area.

If you have not found a designated workspace for your child, that will be step one. The workspace you choose needs to be located where your child can work with minimal distractions. Do not panic if you don't have a large workspace for your child—the space that your child works in does not have to be a big one. In a classroom, your child would typically have a workspace that consists of a desk or section of a table. I don't advocate for buying a desk. You can have your child work on a card table or a section of the kitchen counter, as long as the space provides adequate room for their computer or tablet and any papers, pencils, etc., that they may need to complete their assignments.

If you have more than one child working at home virtually, if at all possible, try to seat your children apart from each other. This will cut down on distractions if they are both working on lessons at the same time.

The survey asked you to assess the background behind your child. The purpose of this is to ensure that there is nothing distracting behind your child. Something that attracts attention will affect your child, as they are seeing their reflection or image on their screen, and it can also affect the other students in the virtual learning environment. For instance, if your child's background opens to a busy area of your home where people are passing by the camera, your child's attention will go to who is walking behind them, as will the attention of the other students in the class who are watching. A way to address this is to use virtual backgrounds. Virtual backgrounds are great—I use them all the time as a way to protect the privacy of my home. You don't want to have to worry about having those who are viewing your child see other people moving in the background, your household possessions, or even if you cleaned house that day!

Success Tip: Using a virtual background helps protect the privacy in your home. You can put a backdrop and affix it to the wall. You can use poster board or a sheet or fabric. You can also download virtual backgrounds that can be saved on your Zoom or Google classroom account. Keep in mind you want it to look professional, so I would not suggest images of forests, beaches, palm trees, lunar surfaces, or the like. Keep it as simple as possible.

Clutter Busters

Setting up a clutter-free workspace and area for your child is optimal. We know that students work better in an organized workspace. If you can get some small organizer bins from a discount or dollar store, these can be helpful accessories.

You don't have to spend a lot of money on designer organizers; you can even use a simple milk carton to create a supply caddy. This is a fun art project that you can do with your kids.

◇◇◇◇◇◇

CREATE A PENCIL SUPPLY CADDY

Here are the steps to creating a pencil holder using a milk carton.

Materials needed:
- Empty half gallon milk carton
- Scissors
- Tape
- Gift wrap
- Pom poms, jewels, other decorative items of choice
- Glue gun
- Ribbon, three-quarters of an inch in width

Instructions:

1. Take the milk carton and rinse it out well. Ensure that it is completely clean and dry.

2. Cut the milk carton down to 4 inches high.

3. Discard the top part of the milk carton.

4. Wrap the carton using the tape and gift-wrapping paper.

5. Using a glue gun, glue the pom poms or other decorations around the milk carton. Let the glue dry completely on decorative objects placed on the carton. This may take about an hour.

6. Glue a ¾-inch-wide piece of ribbon around the carton and tie a bow.

After the ribbon dries, you have a cute container that your child can use for their pencil, pens, and scissors.

◇◇◇◇

Success Tip: Helping your child create their own caddy will build a sense of ownership and pride. Children enjoy creative projects. This is a great opportunity to work together with your child and build collaboration.

In order to keep clutter at bay, ensure you have your child tidy up their workspace each day when they are done with their studies. If this is a daily routine, it will not become a huge chore in the future and will keep the space easy to manage.

Here is a simple checklist you can use with your child to help them with decluttering each day.

◇◇◇◇◇◇

DAILY CLUTTER BUSTER

❑ Pick up any papers and put them in my folder.

❑ Place all my pencils, pens, and scissors in their designated places.

- ❑ Clean and sanitize my worktable. To sanitize, use a product that works to kill germs on surfaces.
- ❑ Check the floor and pick up any garbage.
- ❑ Push in my chair.

Use the daily clutter buster as a checkout for your child when their day of learning is complete. You should notice that after about a week of doing this daily, your child will not need a reminder but will automatically check and declutter their learning space independently.

<><><><>

> **Success Tip:** We suggest reminding your child of the clutter buster after a long weekend or extended holiday from school. Habits can be broken when we are not practicing them daily. After a long break, go over the clutter buster checklist with your child to refresh their memory on the process.

Setting Up the Learning Environment

We have made some good progress so far. You have assessed your environment to determine an appropriate space for your child to work. You have thought about clutter and learned the importance of having a clutter-free area to promote optimal learning. You have learned a routine to use with your child to promote independence in clutter control. You now are at the point where you are ready to set up your learning environment.

Where Should You Set Up the Learning Environment?

I have often been asked to suggest the best place to set up my child's learning space. My advice is to try to stay away from bedrooms and high-traffic areas if at all possible. The drawback to having your child work in a bedroom is that they can easily be distracted, and you want to separate their bedroom, which is a calm space, from their school space.

High-traffic areas are not optimal because your child can be distracted from their learning, and it takes at least two to three minutes to refocus, on average. If you have more than five interruptions, that can add up to fifteen minutes of lost learning time. That is why having a quiet spot with little to no interruptions is optimal.

Below are some pictures of effective workspaces.

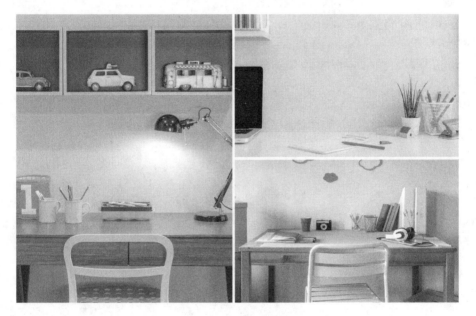

Tools and Materials

Assembling the necessary materials and tools is important to make virtual learning easy for you and your child. The tools and materials you will need include the following:

- Laptop computer, tablet, desktop computer, or other digital tool like a smartphone
- Writing utensils (pencils, pens, crayons, markers, etc.)
- Dictionary, thesaurus, or other reference books

- Paper for writing and taking notes

- Desk or table for working space

- Table lamp or natural light from a window

- Chair that is comfortable for sitting for an extended time

Closing Thoughts on the Learning Environment

Remember to make your learning environment comfortable for you and your family. There is no perfect setup, but the key is to have all the necessary tools readily available, and a well-organized, set place for learning. This will help make concentrating more effortless for your child. Using the tips in this chapter, you can assess your environment and make the right decisions for your home.

CHAPTER 3

WHY ROUTINES MATTER

*"You will **never change your life until you change something you do daily.**"*

—John C. Maxwell

How to Set Up a Winning Routine

Putting a routine in place for your child will save you many hours of heartache and unrest. One of the main tools in a teacher's tool belt is to set up a routine in their classroom. This is taught in all teacher preparation programs because we know that with routine comes order and normalcy. Classrooms with routines set up a natural flow that allows children to know what is coming next, which helps decrease anxiety and builds a sense of calm.

Establishing and adhering to a predictable schedule and routine for your child will help them feel more secure and also will enable you to have an organized morning. In this chapter, we will discuss ways to set up routines that will be easy to follow and will help your child stay focused so that precious learning time is not wasted. This will help to make your morning better organized so you have a better flow.

Nightly Routines

Having nightly procedures or rituals that you follow will make bedtime stress free and enjoyable for you and your child. Think about setting up a nightly routine. This routine should be simple and should be followed each night to build consistency.

Some things to consider in your nightly routine include the activities you will include each night and the order in which they will occur.

Below is a sample nightly procedure that you can tweak to make it work for you.

1. Tidy up. Before getting ready for bed a good practice is to tidy up. This allows your child to get their sleeping environment ready by clearing any clutter that may be in their sleeping space. You can set a timer for 3 to 5 minutes so your child has a time limit to get their area in order. This task will help make the room sleep ready by clearing the environment to prepare for slumber.

2. Take a shower or bath. Taking a shower or bath before bedtime is a way to relax. This is a great way to prepare your child for sleep. Studies have shown that taking a bath before bedtime helps you fall asleep faster.

3. Brush teeth. Have your child brush their teeth before bed. This is a good way to signal that you are winding down for the night and will not be eating or drinking anymore.

4. Read a book. Reading is a great way to relax the mind to prepare to sleep. You can read a bedtime story to your child or, if they are older, they can make it a habit to read something before going to sleep. Numerous studies prove that reading before bedtime can enhance your sleep.

5. Play soothing music. Turn on some soothing music. Lullabies or soft instrumental music can be used to help set the mood for sleep.

6. Turn on the nightlight. If your child has a hard time sleeping in the dark consider getting a nightlight that can be used to cast a faint light in the room. This is also helpful with calming your child so they can prepare to sleep.

7. Tucking in. Tucking in can be a very good way to prepare kids for sleep. They may have a favorite stuffed toy that they like to sleep with. Tucking them in with this stuffed toy is a great way to help your child relax so they can have a good night's sleep.

Pick and choose the tips that will be most useful for you. By having a nightly routine you will not only make be time easier, you will also have time to connect with your child and bond.

A Good Night's Sleep

Having a nightly routine helps children get the necessary sleep they need to be functional for the school day. Studies show that children who follow a consistent nightly routine are more likely to sleep through the night without waking.

We emphasize the necessity for our toddlers to get a good night's sleep, but it becomes even more crucial for our school-age children. Children who have adequate sleep perform better in school and tend to have a more positive mood.

So what is adequate sleep? Doctors recommend that children get at least 10 hours of sleep per night. Teens need at least 8 hours per night. Here is a breakdown of the recommended hours of sleep depending on your child's age.

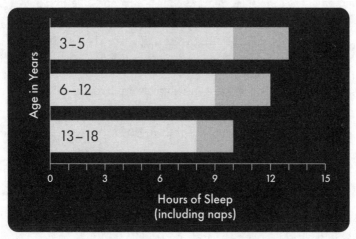

RECOMMENDED SLEEP

Wake-Up Call

Whether your children are attending class in person or due in front of the computer at a certain hour in the morning, setting a specific time for them to wake each day is an important routine to establish. Make sure that their wake-up time is early enough so that they can awaken gently and have time to wash up and eat a leisurely breakfast before starting their school day.

Unfortunately, many of us are used to rushing in the mornings. We keep hitting the snooze button and before we know it, we only have thirty or forty minutes to get ready for work or school and sometimes even less than that. When I was in college, I remember rushing in the morning to get ready for school due to my continuous hitting of the snooze button. I had it down to a science where I could be out the door in half an hour. This is not something to boast about, because it often meant I left important papers at home or had to speed to campus, both of which were not helpful for me.

Rushing in the morning is a bad habit for adults, and we may make it a habit for our children because they often depend on us to wake them up so they can start their day. This is even more common if we have younger children who depend on their parents to wake them and get them ready for school.

> **Success Tip:** Creating a set time that your children wake each morning is a good habit to form. They should wake up the same time on every school morning. On the weekends, sleeping in is OK, but the sleep-in time should be no more than one or two hours later so that their internal alarm is not disturbed.

One important thing to do before moving along in this chapter is to sit down and create a wake-up schedule for you and your family. The following morning wake-up assessment questions can be used to help you get started with your plan.

1. What time do you currently wake in the mornings?   _____

2. How much time does that allow you to get yourself
and your child ready for school and/or work?   _____

3. How would having an additional thirty minutes each morning to meditate or just start the day in a relaxed way make you feel?

_____

_____

_____

4. How would having this relaxed routine help you in your interaction with your family in the morning?

_____

_____

_____

If making more time in the morning would ease your family's routine, consider resetting your wake-up schedule.

The Breakfast of Champions

Breakfast really is the most important meal of the day. Children benefit in many ways when they are able to eat breakfast each morning. Children who eat a balanced breakfast outperform their peers who do not eat breakfast on state assessments, according to many research studies. This shows us that having something to eat each morning will enable your child to focus better on their studies. Think about yourself: I am known to be "hangry" if I do not eat in intervals throughout the day. For years, I skipped breakfast and often found myself in a slump by 9:00 or 10:00 a.m. each morning. This led me to run to the vending machine to fill up on candy and chips. This cycle provided me with quick jolts of energy, but I experienced a crash by lunchtime.

This is the same thing that happens to our children if they do not have something to eat each morning. We wake up from up to eight hours of not eating or drinking, so our bodies need food and water to get going. Answer the following questions to see how you are doing in regard to providing breakfast for your kids each morning.

1. How many times each week does your child eat breakfast? (Every day, most days, never)

_____

2. What does your child typically eat for breakfast?

_____

_____

3. What are some foods that your child likes to eat for breakfast?

_____

_____

4. How much time does it take for your child to eat his/her breakfast? (This question is important, because you want to ensure you give them enough time to eat, but that they start their school day on time.)

_____

5. What are some foods that need to be on hand daily so your children can have a healthy breakfast?

_____

_____

Taking the information from the questions above, fill out the following template.

Breakfast start time:_____ End time:_____

Sample breakfast menus

Monday	Tuesday	Wednesday	Thursday	Friday

Groceries needed for proposed breakfast menu:

Notes:

Fail-Proof Morning Routine

The next step in ensuring your morning routine is fail-proof is to remember that nothing is set in stone. So be flexible with your routine. If you find that your kids need more or less time to get ready in the morning, adjust as necessary. Allowing yourself and your children that grace is really important. We do it at school when we find that certain things are just not working for our students. Give yourself permission to have this same flexibility.

If you see that something is not working and may need adjustment, be sure to sit with your child and explain the change before you implement it. This will help avoid undue anxiety and power struggles. It is also a good idea to elicit feedback and suggestions from your children on the morning routine.

Scheduling the Day

So far, we have a good plan in place for our mornings. The kids have a set time to go to bed and to get up. They have a planned time to eat breakfast. To keep this momentum going, you will need to have a set schedule for the day.

If your children have a schedule that they are supposed to follow from their school, be sure that you understand it fully so you can help your kids follow it. In some schools, students have a set work schedule and meet with the teacher online for their lessons at consistent times, when they are expected to be in their seat for their lessons. This is synchronous teaching, since the teacher is there and can provide immediate feedback to your child.

Some schools just have children meet with their teachers to check in during the day. In this scenario, there is no set scheduled time that they have to log in for specific teaching activities. After the short check-in, students go off to work independently. This model is asynchronous because your child will get feedback at a later time, since most of their work is being done independently.

There are a lot of different models, so your first step is to determine the expectations for the daily schedule.

If you have more than one child, be sure to keep track of each of their schedules so that you stay organized and each child is on time for their individual lessons.

I know that the daily schedule is often a cause for stress. This is especially common when you have more than one learner at home and the school has different lunchtimes and instructional times for different grade levels. To reduce the stress, again be sure that you are clear on the schedules and write them out using a form like the one below. If you find that there is an overlap or a problem with the schedule, reach out to your child's teacher and see if something can be worked out. We will be talking more about the importance of communicating with your child's teacher in Chapter Five. In my experience, maintaining this communication is the best way to stay sane during virtual learning.

> **Success Tip:** Lay out all of your children's schedules and determine if there is any overlap. If there is, reach out to your child's teacher to see if you can make any adjustments. This will head off struggles for you and your family.

What follows is a bare-bones schedule review form. Add all the subjects/classes for each child, their breaks, recesses, and, if they have set study times, add those, too.

Schedule Review

Child's Name: _____

Subject/Time: _____

Break: _____

Lunch: _____

Subject/Time: _____

Dismissal Time: _____

Going with the Flow

Following a flow in your day is my last tip for ensuring you have successful routines in place. A day that flows is one that has set times that work for all parties and make sense for everyone. By this, I mean that if you find that your day is choppy and your kids are sitting around without work to do or have no breaks in between their workday, then your day is not flowing.

Implementing order in the way the school day runs is essential to having a positive virtual learning experience. It is the stuff in the middle that matters most.

We spent the first part of this chapter ensuring that your kids' day starts out positively. We focused on having them get their proper sleep and not have to rush to get their day started.

We then established a routine for breakfast so they are starting their day well fed to fuel their bodies to face their lessons.

We then looked at their schedules to make sure your children are on time and know what to expect during the day.

The last thing to assess is the flow of the day.

If the morning is starting off great, but your child is waning toward the end of the day, be sure to reach out to the school and let them know. There may be some opportunity to build in more breaks or to change the order of the subjects being taught. Some kids do better having independent time first thing in the morning and their direct time with their teacher later in the day. If the school has video-recorded lessons, you may be able to schedule your child to do their subjects at different times of the day, or they can possibly go back in and watch them at later times of the day to support their learning.

The key is to talk with your child and the teacher to find out what will work so they have a positive flow to their day. Most schools will be more than willing to work something out to help make pacing more positive for your child. If you find that there is not much flexibility, then going with the flow will mean something a little different. If this is the case, you will need to work with your child to figure out ways to make the transition from one subject to another more pleasant. You can try using music to transition them from math to reading. One fun thing to do is to come up with a playlist that you use to signal a change from one subject to the next.

Again, the goal is to help your child flow in their day in a meaningful and stress-free way.

> **Success Tip:** Playing music can be a way to signal your child that they are moving from one subject to another. Play a short snippet of a song to indicate the transition.

Closing Thoughts on Routines

I hope the tips in this chapter have helped you think of ways to make your routines manageable and enjoyable. As we note, having a set bedtime and morning routine can help your child perform better in school. I the next chapter, we will talk about techniques to set boundaries with your child if they are struggling with virtual learning. We will offer some ideas for ways to curtail struggles before they happen.

CHAPTER 4

SETTING BOUNDARIES WITH YOUR CHILD

"Boundaries are a part of self-care. They are healthy, normal, and necessary."

—Doreen Virtue

Ready, Set, Go

Congratulations, you have set up an environment that supports learning. Your kids are eating a hearty breakfast and have a set wake-up time. They have a routine that is well thought out and works for your family. Everything should now be smooth sailing, and autopilot should be ready to kick into place, right? The answer is yes and no. You have to make sure you are ready to help your child understand that while they are working at home, they are still technically in school. This can be hard for kids to grasp, especially with so many distractions at home like their favorite pet or a new toy they're fond of.

Parents have told me that one of the biggest struggles they face during virtual learning is how to set boundaries so their kids understand that they need to have the same discipline and focus at home as they would in a physical classroom. In this chapter, we will discuss some ways to help your child adjust to learning at home by establishing some clear guidelines that will allow you to support your child's virtual learning without reaching your wit's end.

Nip Struggles in the Bud by Setting Boundaries

A "boundary" is defined by Merriam-Webster's dictionary as "something that indicates or fixes a limit or extent." In schooling from home, it is vital to set up boundaries with your child so they understand the extent of how their behavior will need to change. We might think that kids will automatically understand the shift in behavior needed to successfully work at home, but the fact is, even as adults, we have to set our own boundaries so that work does not invade our personal spaces.

For instance, if you are working from home and do most of your work in your bedroom, you may find it difficult to sleep at night because you have associated your bedroom with your workspace. Kids often have the opposite challenge. They are likely to associate home with the place they can let their hair down and have fun. So for us to ask them to settle down and work in your house, as they would in school, can be very troubling for them.

In each vignette below, I share a common issue regarding setting boundaries and provide some concrete solutions to help parents respond in appropriate ways.

VIGNETTE 1: My daughter, Marie, is having a very hard time staying focused on her reading lesson. Her mind starts to wander, and then she begins to walk around the house. What can I do?

Solution: If your child is having a hard time focusing on the task at hand, dig deeper to determine if they are having difficulty understanding the task or if they are being defiant. You can do this by having a quick check-in conversation with your child. In education we call it skill versus will. Sometimes children act out because they don't understand a skill or concept. Other times students willfully misbehave to avoid what seems to them an unpalatable task.

If this is a skill deficit, work with your child's teacher to come up with a plan to remediate their learning. If it's a will issue, develop a plan for positive discipline to change the undesired behavior. You can consider offering rewards if the task is completed, and giving consequences if the task is not completed. We'll explore a few of these a bit later in this chapter.

VIGNETTE 2: Fatima is a work-at-home mom with two children, ages seven and ten. Her ten-year-old son keeps going to other websites instead of the ones his teacher has assigned. Fatima has had numerous conversations and has made it clear that staying on the correct websites is the expectation. The behavior stopped for about a week. She thought she was in the clear until she again caught her son on a gaming website instead. What can she do?

Solution: Have a conversation with your children to remind them of the expectations for learning at home. Explain that they are working remotely similar to the way you are. Explain that you each have a job to complete and come up with shared rules that will be followed.

Asking the children to help write the rules is a great way to elicit input to create change.

VIGNETTE 3: Due to an unforeseen school closure, Tom's first-grader Pearl is now working from home virtually. Pearl is having a hard time with being on the computer. She refuses to sit at the computer and runs away. She cries during the entire lesson if she is forced to sit for a lesson. Tom has tried reasoning with Pearl, providing rewards if she sits through the lessons, to no avail. What can he do now?

Solution: In the case of younger children who are struggling with being in an online learning environment, you try cutting down the time that your child is online. Reach out to your child's teacher and see if you can get some work packets that your child can use to supplement the learning. You want to take baby steps when it comes to getting your child more accustomed to being online for extended periods of time. To avoid making this a power struggle be sure to explain to your child that your goal is to have them be online with the rest of the class, but that you understand they are having a hard time with this. Make goals and build on them. For example, if your child can sit through half a lesson, set up a reward. Then make the goal to sit through an entire lesson. Keep upping the goal until your child is able to sit through the entire day. This may take time depending on your child's ability to adjust to the online setting. Ensure you are in communication with your child's teacher so they know the progress you are making in having your child participate fully online.

VIGNETTE 4: Sally says that her son Jerry has been rushing through his work so he can have "free time." His teacher allows students to go on to games and applications when they finish their work. Sally notices that Jerry is rushing through the work and not giving it his best effort. In fact, most of his responses were incorrect. She has constantly told him to slow down, focus, and not just rush through the work.

Solution: In the case of Jerry, start by calling a meeting with Jerry and letting him know that his education is very important. That simply rushing through the assignments is not acceptable and will not prepare him for the concepts that will continually become more complex. Set up a time to meet with Jerry and his teacher to come up with a system that his work has to be completed within a reasonable amount of time with adequate proficiency in order for him to be able to work on games and applications. See how it goes with the new rules. If the behavior continues you might have to take away some of Jerry's free time after school and have him work on some assignments since he is choosing to rush through his assignments and not focus during the school day.

VIGNETTE 5: Steve and Gail are struggling with their daughter Hannah, who is refusing to complete her online work. Hannah is a straight-A student who is very capable of doing the work. She goes to any lengths to avoid working, from saying she is not feeling well to being defiant and saying she will not do the work. They are at a loss as to what to do next.

Solution: In a case like this, where you are dealing with defiance, it is important to immediately set boundaries with your child and let them know that their job is to complete their school work. Explain that as the parent you are account-able for them going to school and learning each day. Have a conversation with your child to find out why they are refusing to do their work. Be an open listener, but again reiterate that the work must be done and that consequences will be given if the defiance continues. Talk about what things would be used as a reward once they begin to get the work done. Make it clear that rewards and/or consequences will depend on your child's actions. In my experience, refusal to work and defiance can stem from another underlying issue. Kids are very sensitive, and it is possible they are stressed from all the changes that are currently occurring in our world.

If the behavior continues you may want to reach out for professional help to ensure that something else is not going on.

Your Words Matter

One tip I give parents is to make sure that you are using positive language with your kids. It is amazing how children's attitudes and behaviors change when we frame our discussions and words in a positive light.

For example, instead of saying "no," you can say "not now" or "maybe later."

Below are some word exchanges you can try with your child:

WORD	EXCHANGED WORDS
No	• Not now. • That is for later. • Hold on a minute.
Stop	• Wait. • Slow down. • Let's try this instead.
Be quiet	• Lower your voice. • Voice level. • Remember we are inside.

Use the following form to write in exchanged words for some of the negative phrases you might find yourself using with your kids.

WORD	EXCHANGED WORDS

What to Do If Your Child Does Not Want to Work

If you tried to follow the advice from the vignettes above, and your child still does not want to work at home, then we need to dig a little deeper and see what is causing that.

First, I would determine whether the work might be too hard or too easy. Kids often shut down if the work is too difficult, and if the work is too simple, they often blow it off and just choose not to do it, or they zip through it quickly without much thought.

The best way to assess if the work is too hard is to look at the task and have your child explain to you how to do it. If they struggle or say they don't know, you might be looking at an assignment that is a little over their head. If they struggle to explain how to complete the task, my suggestion would be to quickly explain the task and see if your child can do the work. If this fails, you can reach out to the teacher and find out if they can give you some support for your child. The teacher may have some time to meet with the child to provide some individual or small group help, or they may be able to give your child some alternative assignments to help them build up to the concept.

The important thing is to work on this as soon as possible so your child gets the extra support they need to be successful.

To see if the work is too easy, ask your child the same question as above. If they are able to explain the concept and even teach you ways to do it more efficiently, chances are the work is a bit below their capabilities. In this case, again reach out to your child's teacher to see if they can offer any alternative work assignments that might hold your child's interest.

You can also assign some activities for your child to complete to challenge them. Below are some fun and easy challenge activities that can be used across content areas.

Challenge activities:

- Write a report.
- Make a game.
- Record a podcast or news story.
- Create a poster board.

> **Success Tip:** If your child is consistently finding assignments either too challenging or too simple, you may want to have a conference with the teacher. Perhaps your child needs an accelerated syllabus or to revisit a previous level. During your conference provide concrete examples of the situation and be prepared to share examples.

As mentioned, another reason your child may not want to work is due to defiance. Many parents find that their kids are struggling with online learning because they are hungering for the structures we have in our schools. To combat this at home, stay the course and maintain those routines and procedures we talked about in the previous chapters.

The key is not to cave in to the pressure to let your child have their way and avoid their work. You will need to put in place some consequences for not getting their work done.

You might consider taking away playtime, limiting use of entertainment devices, etc. Determine what your child enjoys, and let them know access to that depends on their studies. You can allow more or less time on those leisure activities, and possibly take them away if they do not complete their assigned schoolwork.

This can be very stressful at first, as most kids will try to challenge you and get you to give up. Stick with it! Just when you are about to surrender, often the child will be ready to follow the rules and become compliant. They just need to know you mean business and that you are not going to budge.

How to Motivate Your Child

Motivating your child is another great way to help kids that are pushing their boundaries. Children need to see a purpose in what they are doing. In the traditional classroom we do this by making the learning more real world. We talk about how what they are learning today will impact their future. We also accomplish this by providing stories about kids their age who have accomplished tasks that we are getting ready to study. For instance, if you are learning about recycling you can share a story about a child their age who sponsored a recycling project to raise money for charity. Stories such as this create empathy and also spark interest to learn more about the subject since they can see themselves possibly doing something similar one day.

As a parent, you are your child's number one teacher. They look at everything you do and say, and your words of encouragement mean the world to them. Never underestimate the importance of hearing a word of encouragement from you.

Find out what motivates your child and give it to them. Your child may feed off of praise. If so, be sure to offer them words of affirmation at least three to four times a day. If they like to be rewarded, then build in prizes and treats (preferably those that are free, though it's best to avoid food) to reward them. Kids like to hear their favorite song, to go for a walk, or to play a game with you. Be creative, but use these motivators to help your child stay focused on their schooling. If your child feels they are just going through the motions and logging in and completing work, they may soon begin to push their boundaries. Before it starts, curtail this by building in a motivation process in your home. To motivate your tween or teens you can use the suggestions above and also think about giving them free time to explore their interests, Facetime with friends, or have a dance party. Again, these are only suggestions. You know your child best and can determine what they enjoy and what brings them happiness. Build off of these to create motivating moments.

> **Success Tip:** There are many websites that offer virtual field trips. Kids can take an aerial fieldtrip over the Grand Canyon or visit Disneyland and go on a virtual ride. Simply do an internet search and type in "virtual field trips." You will be surprised at how many options arise.

Motivational Tips

Here are some ideas of motivational triggers you can use:

- Set a timer for three times during the school day. When it goes off, give your child a genuine compliment about their work or work ethic.

- Get a jar and put in slips of paper that list different activities you and your child enjoy doing together. At the end of the week, pull from the jar and celebrate by doing one of the activities over the weekend.

- Let your child pick a playlist that you can play when they complete a task that they find difficult.

- Have a fun Friday where you and the kids do something you enjoy for 30 minutes to reward them for a week of hard work. Play board games or go to the park for a picnic.

- Take your kids on a field trip. You can take them to a physical museum or go on a virtual field trip to expand upon something they are learning in class. This is a great way to motivate your kids to learn at deeper levels.

Relaxing Boundaries

I would like to end the chapter with some ideas of ways to sometimes relax boundaries. As with anything, all work and no play make learning dull. There may be times when your child needs to have a more relaxed environment due to stress at home or different situations that are affecting your home life. I give you permission to relax those boundaries and have a "free day" if you need it. The key here is balance. We all know that during these trying times, things sometimes don't go as planned. The internet may go down or you may have to help a family member. Give yourself the permission to take care of your needs and the needs of your family.

> **Success Tip:** If you are having a "relaxed day," be sure to let your child's teacher know, in case there is something that your child will miss, which they'll need to make up at a later time.

Closing Thoughts on Setting Boundaries

As we've seen, it's crucial to establish and enforce boundaries so your children know that learning at home is serious work and not play time—the same rules apply as if they were in the classroom.

You've examined ways to determine why a child might feel unmotivated, and I've given you some ideas on how you can provide incentives—both positive and negative—for home students to take virtual learning seriously. I am confident these ideas will provide effective measures you can use at home to make learning more enjoyable and not a power struggle.

CHAPTER 5

COMMUNICATING WITH YOUR CHILD'S TEACHER

*"Seek first to understand and
then to be understood."*
—Stephen R. Covey

Working with your child's teacher will be important when maneuvering virtual learning. If you have open lines of communication with your child's teacher(s), the process of learning from home will be a lot smoother. In this chapter, we will discuss ways to ensure open lines of communication. We will provide some questions to ask and some good strategies to know on how to stay current and on the same page with your child's teacher.

All Questions Are Good Questions

Many parents are not sure what questions they should be asking their child's teacher. I suspect they may be afraid to ask the wrong questions. I want to encourage you to think about the areas you have concerns about, and then prepare to ask your child's teacher those questions. In this chapter we will discuss ways to prepare to talk with your child's teacher, we'll address some common questions, and we'll come up with a game plan to maintain open lines of communication.

Remember that there are no bad questions. If you need clarity on something, never hesitate to ask. Often the questions you think you should know the answers to are important questions that possibly the teacher and the school did not anticipate.

Sometimes parents are reluctant to ask questions because they may think that the question is not a good one, or that it is something they should already know. First of all, asking for clarity is a sign of intelligence. You are not expected to know everything, and your child's teacher is there to help you.

As noted, sometimes schools and teachers do not know what they need to communicate to parents. Educators sometimes make assumptions; therefore, when you, as a parent, ask questions, you can get a pulse on what you need more clarity on or seek more help with—for instance, if you have a question about how to assist your child with a particular strategy or lesson. By asking your child's teacher for support, they can recognize where they may need to be clearer with their directions. You are actually helping out the teacher by asking questions. Your questions serve as the teacher's mirror for what they may need to change or clarify in their virtual classrooms.

> **Success Tip:** As with you and your child, virtual instruction is also new to many teachers. They are very likely honing their lessons, plans, and approach, and most would truly welcome your feedback.

What Is Your Child's Teacher Expecting from You?

Many parents wonder what their child's teacher expects from them regarding communication. The most valuable input the teacher wants in terms of communication is honesty. As we stated earlier, your comments and feedback are a mirror for the teacher to monitor and adjust their practices to best meet the needs of your children.

By providing open and honest communication about what you need, and what you don't understand, the teacher can better home in on what they are doing or how they are presenting it so that less confusion occurs. An example of this was when I taught kindergarten many moons ago. One of the parents would stop by most mornings to ask for clarification about my homework assignments. By her coming by and giving me feedback, I was soon able to see that I was not providing clear instructions that parents could use to help their children complete the homework packets. Her honest comments and questions helped me to monitor my practice and improve on the instructions I included with my weekly homework packets. After a few test runs and her helpful input, I was soon able to send out homework that was clear, and parents were thrilled with the results. Had this parent not communicated her need, I would not have been able to make this change, which benefited all of my classes' parents and students.

This shows that if you have a question, it's likely that many other parents have the same question. By asking for clarification, you are assisting all parents in the classroom.

Another thing that your child's teacher expects from you is that you look at their daily or weekly communications. Be sure to check those before asking questions. That way, you can avoid covering topics that may have already been addressed in the newsletter or online post. These days, most teachers are using online apps to communicate with parents. The beauty in this is that up-to-date information can be shared in real time. If you are not sure where to find these communications, reach out to your child's teacher so they can show you where the posts are located.

> **Success Tip:** Be sure to check the daily and/or weekly communications that your child's teachers provide. These will allow you to be in the know regarding any changes in the daily schedule, subject matter, assignments, and so on.

Ensure that when there are events, whether virtual or in person, that you make the time to attend them. This is a great way to keep communication channels open. At these live events, you are able to have an audience with your child's teacher as well as the opportunity to connect with other parents.

How to Avoid Conflict with Your Child's Teacher

I am including this section on avoiding conflict with your child's teacher as a resource—I hope you will not have to use it. Conflicts can sometimes arise when we have a difference of opinion, miscommunication, or personality clashes. Whatever the reason for the conflict, you can avoid it by being up front with your child's teacher and letting him or her know if you have issues that you need clarified or that you feel are not being addressed. Virtual learning can be stressful for all parties. There is also an element of disconnect that you have to work through. If you are not able to meet your child's teacher in person and mainly communicate virtually, that can be very difficult as it can sometimes lead to misunderstanding or miscommunication. If you are a person who prefers face-to-face communication, you can request an in-person meeting or a virtual meeting so that you can see your child's teacher visibly.

> **Success Tip:** Communicate as soon as an issue arises so that problems are quickly assessed and taken care of. Request a meeting in the format that you find most favorable to make the interaction more successful. Many issues can be solved with a quick conversation.

Don't Stew over Things

Another tip to avoid conflict is not to let things stew. If you have a small issue, it is better to address it immediately so it does not turn into something bigger.

As a parent, I always connected with my child's teacher if I saw something that might potentially become an issue in the future. For example, my son once had a teacher who gave a lot of homework assignments to be done each night for the next morning. I was able to explain our situation with sports and other scheduling conflicts, so we got permission for him to turn in his homework at the end of each week. This actually turned out to be helpful for most parents, and the policy was changed for the entire class. In this instance, I knew that there would be difficulty getting the homework done, and by reaching out to the teacher and explaining the situation, we were able to come to a compromise.

> **Success Tip:** It never hurts to talk to other parents of children in your child's class, if something doesn't feel right to you. Another parent may also be experiencing the same difficulties as you are. That will give you added confidence when you speak to the teacher.

Finding Common Ground

Another way to build a relationship with your child's teacher is to find common ground. Determine what they have a passion for in their classroom. This will allow you to understand the focus they have so you can discover what they value. I am confident you will find that you share many of the same values. Finding this mutual understanding is the first step in building common ground. To begin, take the time to have a casual conversation with your child's teacher. The goal is to talk about your child in a relaxed manner and to get to know the teacher's approach and goals. Here are some questions to guide the conversation:

1. What is your teaching style?

2. What do you consider most important when teaching children?

3. How can I support your work as a teacher?

4. What is important for my child to learn this year?

5. How will you make sure my child's learning preferences are incorporated in your lessons?

6. If you could tell parents one thing about yourself, what would that be?

As you see, the questions are open-ended and will allow your child's teacher to reflect on their practice and share their thoughts in a nonthreatening way. From the information you obtain, you will be able to understand what your child's teacher holds important when it comes to both teaching and learning. No one goes into teaching with the intent of doing a poor job. Teachers have some of the biggest hearts as they dedicate their lives to helping young people. The sweat and tears of every moment of my two decades as a classroom teacher were worth it. I know that I impacted the lives of my students, and that my impact will have a lasting effect. By tapping into this with your child's teacher, you will be able to create that common ground that will propel you forward.

Closing Thoughts on Communication

Virtual teaching can be stressful for both parents and teachers; understanding that we are all doing our best to provide a quality educational experience is important. Communication is going to be pivotal as we work virtually. To avoid feeling isolated reach out often to clarify questions that arise.

Keep the lines of communication open and free-flowing. This will ensure you are in the know about what is happening in the classroom, and that your child's teacher is aware of your concerns so that solutions can be quickly implemented.

CHAPTER 6

TECHNICAL DIFFICULTIES AND ONLINE LEARNING

"Technology can become the 'wings' that will allow the educational world to fly farther than ever before—if we will allow it."

—Jenny Arledge

In this chapter, we will talk about one of the biggest struggles with online learning: technical difficulties. I am sure you have been kicked out of an online program or have found that a program will not run on your child's computer. There is nothing more frustrating than having these issues come up right before a class is starting or in the middle of a lesson.

Believe me, I have had my share of technical difficulties, and I know the stress they can cause. This chapter will provide some steps you can take when you experience those inevitable tech problems.

What to Do When You Can't Get a Program to Work

One of the most common problems I see is when students and parents can't get a program to run. This is often something you can easily solve by reaching out to your child's school so that they can direct you to the correct person to assist with program difficulties. Most schools have a technical support department that can quickly walk you through the process. There is a plethora of reasons why programs run into problems. It can be something on your end, like connectivity issues, but most often it's a system issue on the school's server. With so many students working online, the amount of user traffic sometimes causes bandwidth overload, which can slow down the program. And sometimes the system goes down for scheduled program maintenance. Though this is usually done after hours, there are times when this may occur during the school day. I advise you to be prepared for program glitches and seek help as needed.

> **Success Tip:** When you encounter difficulties with computer programs, stay calm. In fact, if you're not in a huge hurry, sometimes just giving the computer a bit of time allows things to correct themselves. If not, then call the school and seek support as needed.

How to Troubleshoot on Your Own

Sometimes we are just not able to reach technical support in a timely manner, so knowing a few troubleshooting tips and tricks can be very helpful.

A good starting point is to make sure that you have the correct password to the program or the computer. This is a common error, and the solution couldn't be more simple.

Next, be sure that you have selected the correct network connection. This can trip you up if you have a few different wireless connections. I have run into this problem in my own home. We have more than one network, and one is stronger than the other. I often find that when things are lagging, my computer is connected to the incorrect network.

When all else fails, reboot. My son, who works in IT, says that many problems can be solved with this simple solution. Turn the computer off and back on again. This may refresh the connection, clear the memory, and reset programs.

> **Success Tip:** If you intend to restart the computer, make sure that you've saved anything that you can. You don't want your child to lose any work in the process. I try to remember to save after every paragraph when I am writing to ensure I do not lose any of my work.

Digital Citizenship

Digital citizenship refers to exhibiting proper behavior when working online. You can support this by talking to your child about the importance of being kind and considerate when interacting with their classmates over the internet. Cyberbullying can be a major issue for students. I have seen unkind comments in the chat bar on different platforms. Teachers look at these chats and respond appropriately, but to do your due diligence at home, have a conversation with your child about the importance of treating people kindly and being polite when responding to questions and writing online.

> **Success Tip:** In addition to instilling good online citizenship in your child, try to make them feel comfortable talking to you, if they encounter children who are bullies. You might establish a confidential connection with a teacher or administrator to let them know if you have heard about abusive online behavior.

Cybersecurity

Keeping our kids safe when they are online is of great importance. We have all heard about the dangers that can lurk on the web. I am not including this section to scare you, but to provide you with some tips you can use to help keep your kids safe as they are working online.

Be sure that you have a serious conversation with your child about making sure that they know who they are talking with when working online. Set boundaries about the time of day that they can work online, and monitor their online conversations. These three actions should give you a good handle on your child's online activity.

You can use the terms "who," "when," and "where" to monitor online activity. The following graphic can help you keep tabs on your child's encounters on the web.

WHO	WHEN	WHERE
Who is your child talking online with?	When is your child online? What is the time of day that your child is supposed to be online?	Where is your child working? Ensure your child is working in a place where you can see what they are doing online.

Online Learning Platforms

There are numerous online learning platforms that schools use to teach their students. Some of the more popular ones are Blackboard, Canvas, Google Classroom, and Zoom. Each has a different purpose. For example, Zoom and Google Meet are mainly used for meetings. Blackboard and Canvas are often used for students to post their work assignments. Be sure to familiarize yourself with whatever platform or program that your child's school uses. You can request a training session from your child's teacher, or most programs have YouTube videos available online that explain how to use them.

It is important that your child also understands how to use the platforms, of course. You should go over the key functions like how they can mute themselves, raise their hand, and any other function that would be useful when working online. We mentioned the chat feature earlier. Both Zoom and Google Classroom have a chat feature. Be sure your child knows how to use it, as many classrooms use chat for communicating and interacting during real-time sessions.

Trends in Online Learning

As we continue to grow in our understanding of how to teach and learn virtually, we continue to see new trends in online education. My word on this is to make sure that you are in constant communication with your child's school and teacher. What works in one school may not work in your child's school. Ensure that you are up to date on what the expectations are for your child, and don't compare the education that is happening in your friends' or relatives' schools in other areas. Each school has different demographics, curricula, and a plethora of other circumstances that dictate how they run their virtual academies. If you keep this in mind, you won't be swayed by all the latest trends and will stay the course to ensure your child is getting the best education possible.

Closing Thoughts on Technical Difficulties

In some ways, virtual learning is the same as physical classroom learning, and in some ways it's very different.

First, you and your child need to conquer any technical challenges: successfully logging in, getting programs to run smoothly, and making sure your internet connection is quick and reliable. That sets it apart from in-school learning. Also, you want to monitor your child's access to the web in the same way you might keep an eye on where they might physically go after school or between classes.

However, it is very much like attending a traditional school in the way that you want to instill in your child an attitude of respect for other children and for the teacher. And, like in the physical schoolyard, bullying should not be tolerated. Finally, keep in close communication with your child's school and teacher, as they will be pivotal in ensuring you are in tune with the learning expectation.

CHAPTER 7

STRATEGIES FOR MATH

"Mathematics is not about numbers, equations, computations, or algorithms: it is about UNDERSTANDING."

—William Paul Thurston

Let's Talk Math

This chapter will provide you with some easy techniques and strategies that you can do at home with your child to ensure they are kept up to date on their math skills. Math instruction is logical, and the tips we will share can be used casually throughout the day to help enhance your child's math skills. Familiarity creates ease. As you incorporate practicing math problems as part of your home routine, your child will become familiar with the concepts and will have less anxiety when asked to solve them. Because math concepts build on one another from year to year, it is essential that previous math skills be refreshed, so your child does not have to relearn the concepts.

When teaching math, using manipulatives or concrete objects is a great way to make the learning more meaningful for younger students. The chapter is divided by grade-level bands so you can ensure you are using the most appropriate strategy to meet your child's need. Most of the activities can be done at home to keep math concepts alive for your child in a meaningful way. We know that learning math online can be hard for some students. These tips provide easy ways to practice key math content and enhance your child's math skills.

Why Is Math Important?

A sound understanding of basic math concepts is a skill that your child will use for a lifetime. We employ math constantly in our everyday lives. When we are cooking, we're using measurements. When we are shopping, we're using percentages, multiplication, division, and subtraction. Need to figure out a tip at the restaurant? Again, percentages. If your home is being renovated, you are using geometry to figure out the square footage. There is just no getting away from math in our daily lives. Children who are not given a basic foundation in math concepts are at a disadvantage in the everyday world.

In this chapter, we will share some techniques you can use at home to work with your children on the key math skills they will be responsible for at their given grade level. Many of these tips can be practiced with common objects around the house.

Pre-K Math

Prekindergarten children are very inquisitive. They have a thirst for learning and absorb at very quick rates. If you have ever talked to a two- or three-year-old, you are often amazed at how much they actually know about math. I remember talking to my niece about her birthday party, and she was able to explain how she was going to split her candy with her sister so they each had the same amount. This was coming from a three-year-old!

Kids can learn a lot more than we often give them credit for. Be sure to encourage your pre-K child to explore math around the house, and talk to them about numbers. You will be surprised at how quickly they pick it up.

Blocks and Shapes

Playing with blocks and shapes is a great way to create number sense for your pre-K child. When watching young children play with blocks, we notice that they separate them by like shape, they often build what they see in our natural world, and they often can name the shapes like a star or a triangle.

If you have building blocks at home, bring them out and talk to your child about the blocks. You can have some great conversations about math during these talks. The key is to make the conversations natural and child friendly. We want to instill a love of math in students as they see how it connects with their world.

Knowing the names of the shapes is something we teach in kindergarten, but many pre-K students already know what a star, diamond, square, and circle are. You can talk to your child about these shapes when you see them around your environment. Children pick up vocabulary and concepts intuitively when they interact with them in their natural settings. Just a quick statement like, "John, did you see the star on the tree?" goes a long way in teaching math vocabulary.

Learning to Count

Students in pre-K will need to work on their number sense. This will include learning to count to at least ten and to match their counting to items. For example, they should be able to show you one apple or two dogs. You can work on these basic skills by counting with your child every day. Make it a game to count to ten each day. Then gradually start showing your child what the number one represents with objects. You can hold up one toy car and say, "This is one car." Ask your child: "How many cars are there?" And then respond: "There is one car." Keep practicing this until your child is comfortable with the concept, and then move on to representing two items, then three, up until ten.

Rote counting aloud is another activity that your pre-K child should be practicing on a regular basis. Encourage them to count aloud when you are driving in the car or waiting in line. You can also count when you are washing your hands or cooking something in the microwave or toaster. Build in writing whenever possible to provide this important practice for your child. See "Writing Numbers," just ahead, for more information.

> **Success Tip:** Pre-K children should be counting aloud on a frequent basis. Whenever there is down time, practice counting with your child to improve their math skills. Link this to tangible, everyday objects: for instance, on a trip to the supermarket, ask them how many cars they can count in the parking lot, how many apples and oranges they see in the produce section, and so on.

Books about Counting

One of the best ways to teach children about counting is to read counting books together. Including counting books in your reading routine helps to reinforce counting and literacy skills—two very important building blocks of learning. There are so many counting books to choose from. They provide students with colorful characters and engaging scenarios. One of my favorites is *Five Little Monkeys Jumping on the Bed* by Eileen Christelow. You can use the hand motions to engage participation while reading the book. This is a great way to build number sense and practice counting with your child. It is a fun game, and the book is adorable.

I have listed other counting book suggestions in the Appendix on page 143.

Writing Their Numbers

Students in pre-K can begin learning to write their numbers up to five. You can support this by getting a blank piece of paper and making dots for your child to trace the numbers. As they trace the number one, say the number aloud so they associate the number with its written representation. Another tip is to make dots for the numbers in sequence from one to five. Point to each dotted number and say the number aloud. Then, as your child traces the number, have them say each number.

K–1 Math

Students in kindergarten and first grade also work on number sense, but they begin to move into more substantive math concepts like addition and subtraction. As with pre-K students, children in kindergarten and first grade are also very intuitive and pick up on a lot of math concepts from their environment. Talk with your child about math in your world. You can have them help you sort the canned goods before you put them in the cabinet, or have them help you count out the number of items you will need for a recipe. The trick is to talk about math with your child anytime the opportunity arises.

Number Sense

With a strong foundation in number sense, your child will quickly move through the math continuum. Your child will not develop number sense by just circling the correct answer on a worksheet. Number sense develops when students can see and feel the math. This happens when you allow your child to interact with math in the real world. We know that virtual learning has its benefits, but one of its deficits is that children are not able to always work with math blocks and other manipulatives to model what they are learning. Therefore, sometimes it may be up to you to guide your child to work with real objects as a key for building number sense.

Easy ways to do this are to ask your child to show you ten of something if you are working on the number ten. Or if you are working on addition, have them model two plus three by using two buttons and three toothpicks to represent the math problem. The key is to get your kids to feel the math by letting them demonstrate it by using objects.

Writing Their Numbers

Practice writing the numbers with your child. As we noted in the pre-K section, number writing is an important part of math literacy. Kindergarten and first grade students should be able to write numbers up to twenty. At this age level, direct your child to write their numbers on lined paper for practice. You can start out using dots and have them trace them as they are learning how to write the numbers. Take this scaffold away as they become more familiar with the written numbers. Continue with the dots until they are able to write the numbers independently without mistakes.

Counting

As with younger children, one quick routine you can establish with your child is to count daily. Counting helps your child build a sense of numbers and eventually provides them with an understanding of how to manipulate these numbers to perform math tasks. As your child gets more skilled in counting, they will begin to skip count by twos, fives, and tens. These skills will help when they move into multiplication and division in later grades.

To make counting more meaningful, invite your child to move objects while they count. One fun way is to use an egg carton and beans. Your child can put the beans into the egg slots as they count their beans.

Second- and Third-Grade Math

Students in the second and third grades begin to build on the basic number sense they have obtained from first grade. The concepts quickly advance, especially in third grade. Here are some ways to support your child at home.

Reading and Writing Numbers

Although, we are working in the virtual learning environment, it is important that your child know how to write their numbers correctly from one to one hundred and beyond. Be sure to have your child practice writing their numbers. I have seen many students struggle with writing the higher numbers in the hundreds and thousands. Check with your child's teacher to see which numbers they are expected to write and be sure to practice them at home.

It is also important that your child can read their numbers up to one hundred and beyond. This is going to be key when they encounter math problems with higher numbers. A simple way to assess this is to make flash cards out of index cards and test your child's ability to read the numbers. Believe me, this skill is going to be extremely important as your child moves up in the grade levels. You do not want them to struggle with reading numbers, as this will severely affect their understanding of math problems.

Addition and Subtraction

Students will begin to work on addition and subtraction of two-digit numbers with regrouping. This can be very difficult for students to understand if they do not have the important number sense we emphasized in kindergarten and first grade. When you are at home, make up word problems using common objects around the house to practice addition and subtraction. An example would be to ask your child if they have two cans of beans and three cans of pears, how many cans do they have in all? You will adjust the problems based on your child's grade level, but the object is to get your child to think about addition and subtraction in familiar settings.

SAMPLE ADDITION PROBLEM

If you have three oranges and four apples, how many pieces of fruit do you have in all?

SAMPLE SUBTRACTION PROBLEM

If I have nine glowing candles and I blow out four, how many lit candles are left?

Multiplication

Multiplication is a very important skill that your second and third grader will need to master. Multiplication is repeated addition. Students can learn their multiplication fact tables as a way to build multiplication fluency. You can support this at home by using index cards to make multiplication flash cards. I would suggest making flash cards for tables beginning with one and ending with twelve. For instance, you would make cards that were for 1 x 1 up to 1 x 12, and then up to 12 x 12. To build fluency, have your child practice the tables daily. Make it like a game so it's fun for them! You can also consider giving your child prizes for mastering their multiplication facts.

As math does not come easy to every student, it's more important than ever to develop your child's basic skills at home so they will have an easier time in their virtual learning space.

Division

Students often struggle with division when it is first introduced to them. Here are some tips to help your child learn division. First, introduce your child to the different symbols that are used to represent division. Share the following division symbols: ($\div$, /, and -), and on index cards, write the same division problem using each of the symbols. For examples, $6 \div 2$; $6/2$; $\frac{6}{2} = 3$. Explain to your child that although there are different symbols being used, we are still performing the division operation. This is an important statement to emphasize, as your child will need to understand that although a different symbol may be used, the same math operation is expected.

Other practical ways to support division practice at home include acting out division problems using props. I love to use stories to represent division problems. An example of this is to create a story about sharing something and asking your child to figure out how much each person will get. For instance: Caleb has twelve cars to share with his four friends. How many cars will each friend get? You can act this out by using toy cars and having your child put the cars into different piles to represent their friends. Fun activities like this are great to introduce division in a fun way.

As with multiplication, division can be hard to model when working virtually; that is why doing these concrete activities at home is a great way to build understanding.

Fractions

Fractions are one of the most difficult concepts that students need to master. Fractions do not go away, and they become increasingly difficult as we move up in the grade levels. An important concept kids need to understand about fractions is that they represent numbers. Here are some tips you can use at home to help your child understand fractions.

As you support your child with learning fractions, look at familiar ones like ½ to begin the observation. Kids are familiar with one-half of something. To build on this, start to talk about fractions of items. For example, if you have twelve cars and you give your friend six of them, you have given them one-half of the cars. If you have twelve colored pencils and give your friend one-third, you have given them four, and so on.

By making the fractions reflect real life, your child will understand the concept at a deeper level.

FRACTION ART

One fun way to look at fractions is to make a fraction art project. An example would be to ask your child to make a flower, and the petals would represent fractions. If they make a flower with four petals, each petal would be labeled ¼. If they make a flower with six petals each petal would be labeled ⅙.

Example

These are two ways to begin to make fractions more concrete for your child. For other ideas, look in the math resources section in the Appendix.

Telling Time

Telling time to the hour and minute is a skill that is mastered by the end of third grade. To practice this, work with your child on telling time using an analog clock. We have become very accustomed to digital clocks, but it is still important that your child can read an analog clock. You can make a clock with your child as a fun art activity. Here are the directions.

◇◇◇◇◇◇

MAKING A PAPER CLOCK

Materials needed:
- Paper plate
- One brad
- Scissors
- Marker
- Construction paper

Step 1: Take the paper plate and punch a hole in the center using scissors.

Step 2: Cut out a minute hand and hour hand from the construction paper.

Step 3: Place the minute and hour hands on the paper plate using the brad. Put it in the hole that you punched in Step 1.

Step 4: Use a marker to write the numbers around the clock. Start by writing 12 and 6 in their proper positions and then fill in the rest.

Note that you can also use a thumbtack or push pin instead of a brad.

◇◇◇◇

Fourth- and Fifth-Grade Math

As students enter fourth and fifth grade, the level of understanding they will need in mathematics increases swiftly. They begin to work on regrouping, place value, two-digit numbers, decimals, division and ordering, and comparing fractions. In this section, we will discuss some tips you can use with your fourth and fifth graders to ensure they are getting support at home to enhance their mathematical understanding for virtual learning.

Addition and Subtraction with Regrouping

At this level, students will begin to work on addition and subtraction problems that require regrouping. Regrouping refers to making groups of ten to carry out an addition or subtraction problem. Examples would be the following:

$$
\begin{array}{rr}
347 & 80 \\
+\ 123 & -\ 24
\end{array}
$$

In both examples, students will regroup by ten to perform the operation.

In the first problem, $347 + 123$, you will start by adding 7 and 3, which equal 10. You will keep the 0 in the ones place and move the 1 up to the tens place above the 4. This is an example of regrouping. You will add $1 + 4 + 2$, which equals 7. You will then add $3 + 1$, which equals 4. Your final total is 470. In this first example, we had to regroup from the ones place.

In the second example, we will regroup in a subtraction problem. We are subtracting 24 from 80. We start by seeing we cannot subtract 4 from 0, so we need to borrow 1 from the 8. The 8 becomes a 7, and the 0 becomes a 10. We then subtract 4 from 10, which is 6. Then we subtract 2 from 7, which is 5. Our final answer is 56. In this example, we regrouped when we moved 1 over from 8.

When working through problems like this it is important to talk about the math problems as you are solving them.

These models can be used to help support the math that was just explained.

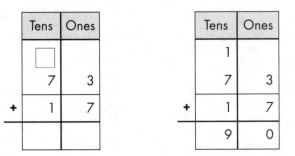

Tens	Ones
☐	
7	3
+ 1	7

Tens	Ones
1	
7	3
+ 1	7
9	0

To support regrouping, you can have your child use base-10 blocks to model the mathematical operation. I would also suggest asking your child's teacher if they can let you use some base-10 blocks to help support your child at home. If they cannot accommodate you, base-10 blocks are sold in most teacher supply stores, or you can purchase them online.

With the base-10 blocks, have your child move the blocks to signify regrouping. An example would be to have them use blocks to model adding. To add 24+17 you would start by putting 2 base ten blocks in the tens place. (See the example on page 70.) You would put 4 ones in the ones place. To represent 17 you would put 1 ten block in the tens column and 7 ones in the ones column.

Start by counting your ones. You have 11 ones. Put one tens block in the tens place, which leaves you with 1 one.

Add up the tens. You have 4, and you have 1 one. The total is 41.

By using the tens blocks your child can have a more concrete understanding of regrouping. You can use the blocks to represent different math problems as you see necessary.

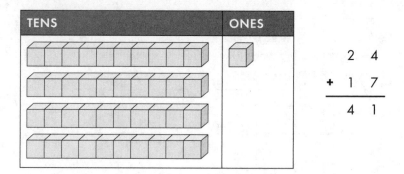

Place Value

Place value is another important skill for fourth and fifth graders. Help your child to create a place value chart like the one below so they can use it as a resource when they are working on math problems.

PLACE VALUE

One Million		Hundred Thousands	Ten Thousands	One Thousands		Hundreds	Tens	Ones
2	,	4	3	8	,	2	0	1

Understanding place value will continue to be important as your child works on decimals, fractions, and eventually, algebra. Place value is taught in the primary grades, but as the numbers become more complex, it is important that students know what value the number has, based on its position. In middle school, place value helps students with regrouping and multi-digit division. This shows how these concepts build on each other, and this skill is important as students move up in their learning.

Decimals

Decimals are another math concept that students encounter in fourth and fifth grades. I can remember having misconceptions about decimals when I was a fifth grader. This is another of the enduring concepts that students will encounter as they move up in their grade levels. Here are a few strategies you can use to help your child master decimals.

Writing Decimals in Different Forms

Understanding decimals requires that children know standard, word, and expanded forms. Standard form refers to the number being written in figures. Word form is, as it sounds, when we write out the decimal number as a word. Expanded form refers to showing the sum of values. Here are these concepts illustrated.

DECIMAL: PLACE VALUE

Hundreds	Tens	Ones		Tenths	Hundredths	Thousandths
8	3	9	.	4	6	5

Standard Form: 839.465

Word Form: Eight hundred thirty-nine and four hundred sixty-five thousandths

Expanded form: $8 \times 100 + 3 \times 10 + 9 \times 1 + 4 \times \frac{1}{10} + 6 \times \frac{1}{100} + 5 \times \frac{1}{1000}$

or

$$800 + 30 + 9 + \frac{4}{10} + \frac{6}{100} + \frac{5}{1000}$$

Note: The further LEFT of the decimal, the larger the value. The further RIGHT of the decimal, the smaller the value.

Ask your to child practice writing decimals in standard, written, and expanded forms. This is a great way to solidify their understanding of decimal concepts. You can also ask them to tell you the value of numbers using different forms when you encounter numbers in magazine articles, newspapers, etc. Keeping these ideas fresh is a great way to instill the learning into your child's permanent memory.

Rounding

Rounding to the nearest ten is important for students to understand. These skills can be used to help them figure out the price of an item or to estimate the answer to a problem. Estimation is a skill we use frequently in our daily lives. When we are buying items in the store, we often round their amounts so we make sure we have enough money to make the purchase.

Rounding is first introduced in third grade, and by fourth grade, your child should be proficient in this. Here are the rules for rounding to the nearest ten.

ROUNDING TO THE NEAREST TEN

STEP 1: Look at the number.

STEP 2: Find the place, for instance ones, tens, or hundreds.

STEP 3: If the number is five or more, add one more place. If it is four or less, let it rest.

ROUNDING

Find the PLACE

Look NEXT DOOR

5 or bigger ADD 1 MORE $^{+1}$

4 or less let it REST stay!

Nearest Ten

42	67	9	4	257
40 stays!	70^{+1}	10 $^{+1}$	0 stays!	260 $^{+1}$

Nearest Hundred

223	658	37	89	2776
200 stays!	700^{+1}	0 stays!	100^{+1}	2800^{+1}

Dividing with Two-Digit Divisors

Long division with two-digit divisors can be tricky for fourth- and fifth-grade students. This concept will be necessary to understand and master as they move up in their math classes. Check with your child's teacher to find out how they teach this concept so you can support your child at home. Have your child practice with single-digit division (10 ÷ 2) as a warm-up, and move on to division problems with two-digit divisors (500 ÷ 25). Practicing these types of problems will help your child become more comfortable with two-digit division.

If you find that your child is struggling, immediately contact the teacher so you can get extra support from the school.

Fractions

Fractions tend to be a challenging concept for some students to grasp. Fractions will not go away as children progress and will be referenced in all future math courses. Ensuring your child has a strong foundation and understanding of fractions is pivotal. In fourth and fifth grade, students are asked to order and compare fractions. Ordering fractions refers to setting them up from least to greatest values. Students order fractions so they can see which fraction has the smallest value and which is larger. This is sometimes done using a number line.

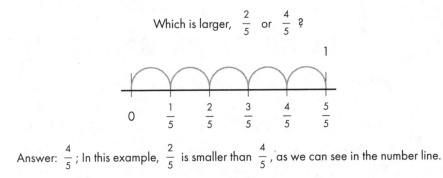

Which is larger, $\frac{2}{5}$ or $\frac{4}{5}$?

Answer: $\frac{4}{5}$; In this example, $\frac{2}{5}$ is smaller than $\frac{4}{5}$, as we can see in the number line.

Comparing fractions refers to looking at two fractions and determining which one is greater. Ordering and comparing fractions is synonymous. You order fractions by putting them in order typically from least to greatest. To determine this, you look at the numerator and compare them to see which is larger.

Here is an activity you can do at home to support understanding ordering and comparing fractions.

◇◇◇◇◇◇

ORDERING AND COMPARING FRACTIONS

Materials needed:

- Index cards
- Pencil or pen

Step 1: Write fractions with the same denominator on index cards.

Step 2: Tell your child you want them to line up the fractions from least to greatest.

Step 3: Watch your child line up the fractions.

Step 4: Go over your child's answers. If there are any errors, ask them to repeat the exercise and fix the order.

Step 5: Tell your child it is now their turn to write their own fractions to line up.

Step 6: Give your child blank index cards to write five fractions.

Step 7: Line up the fractions together with your child from least to greatest. As you line them up, discuss your reasoning.

◇◇◇◇◇◇

Middle School Math

Middle school math involves learning to solve mathematical problems that are increasingly more complex. Written-out problems will begin to become more commonplace. We'll cover reading and comprehension, also critical skills, in the next chapter. That skill is also needed for written math problems. The basic math operations of adding, subtracting, multiplying, and dividing will involve working with larger numbers. In this section we will provide strategies to help your child maneuver middle school math in the virtual learning environment.

Fractions

As we noted in the fourth- and fifth-grade section, fractions will continue to be an area of focus in math as students move up in the grade levels. Middle school students should have a firm grasp on how to order and compare factions. They will now be expected to apply their knowledge of fractions to algebraic thinking. Solving word problems that include fractions is common in middle school. Problems written out as text are not new, but if your child struggles with a basic understanding of fractions, it can be daunting when they encounter such word problems.

To support fractions in the middle school grade level, have your child practice solving fraction word problems on a weekly basis. You can find word problems online or ask your child's teacher for some that you can practice with at home. Here is an example of a fraction word problem.

Katya has ordered a 12-inch pizza, and it was delivered sliced in eight slices. Her three friends Jenny, Cindy, and Anita are visiting. How many slices will each person get?

Providing extra practice for your child will make word problems, and specifically word problems that use fractions, less intimidating.

Geometry

Geometry is the area of math that focuses on shapes and lines. Students begin to learn about more complex geometry concepts in middle school as a way to prepare them for high school geometry. Geometry is one of those math subjects that students either love or hate. I was an excellent geometry student, but I did not necessarily care for algebra. Support your child's growing understanding of geometry by reviewing geometry problems at home. You can find sample geometry problems by conducting an online search. I would also suggest asking your child's teacher to provide insight on the type of geometry problems they will be encountering in class. Use some of these as practice for your child. Remember, familiarity creates ease.

> **Success Tip:** If your child is having trouble understanding or mastering geometry, look online. There are a number of geometry workbooks written specifically for middle school students, and you'll also find websites and programs that will help your child sharpen their geometry skills.

High School Math

Once students get to the high school level, it is important that they know how to reach out to their teachers if they encounter any problems with their math concepts.

All those prior years of basic math facts are now going to be of the upmost importance when students are in high school. This is when all of their fundamental math skills are put into play as they begin to solve advanced math problems.

Algebra

Algebra is a subject that ties together the basic math skills and layers those concepts into logical thinking. Algebra uses numbers and symbols to represent equations. If students are not familiar with math concepts, figuring out the unknown variables in algebra can be basically impossible. To further support your child in understanding algebra, encourage them to take an algebra assessment. There are many available online. Using the information from the assessment, you will know which areas they will need extra support in.

You can also have your child's teacher give you an algebra pre-assessment and go over the results with you. The goal is to use the information from the assessment to determine what support skills may be needed to ensure their success in algebra. Remember, algebra is an accumulation of all of the beginning math skills that are taught in elementary school. At this level they are now looking at math in a more abstract way using formulas and letters. Thus, having this assessment data will let you and your child know what skills they need to work on.

Geometry

The concepts of shapes and lines build from elementary school as students learn about different types of triangles and how to measure angles.

There are a lot of theorems and formulas that students will need to memorize to solve geometry problems. Help your child create a quick sheet with the theorems and formulas they will need so they can learn them, become comfortable with them, and apply them when solving math problems. Another tip is to make sure your child knows the geometric shapes and their relationships. Many shapes are related to each other, and if your child knows this, it can make geometry less challenging. For example, squares and rectangles are quadrilaterals, meaning they have four sides.

Quadrilaterals

1. Straight line segments   **2.** Four sides

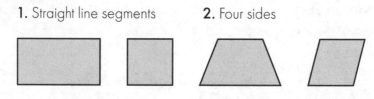

Geometry involving proving things, knowing the angles and their properties, will be useful if they are asked to justify their responses. For example, the sum of angles in a triangle is always 180 degrees. This information will be useful when justifying a solution to a problem that has a triangle.

It is important to know the area and volume formulas as these are found in many geometry problems. By knowing how to quickly find area and volume, your child will be more successful in their math lessons.

Advanced Math Concepts and Courses

If your child is in advanced math classes such as trigonometry or calculus, it is important that they stay on top of their assignments and reach out immediately if they need extra support in any specific areas. Advanced math classes are often accelerated and require a lot of extra time to complete the work. Creating a schedule and sticking to it will be an important step to take.

> **Success Tip:** Virtual study groups are worth looking into if your child is in an advanced math course. Students tend to learn a lot from each other when they are working in study groups. This is especially important when working in virtual learning environments, where it can be isolating. You can look into learning pods, which we mentioned in Chapter 1, as a way to find study partners. Be sure that you have specific ideas on how you want the study sessions to run so your child gets the most benefits from their meetings.

Closing Thoughts on Math

Math literacy is extremely important. Students build on the very basic foundation skills that are introduced as early as kindergarten. The tips and strategies found in this chapter can be used to provide support in key mathematical areas of study. A final tip is to ensure you are in communication with your child's teacher so you can immediately implement support strategies to keep your child on track. Waiting until report cards or parent-teacher conferences will be too late. I suggest checking in on your child's math progress every couple of weeks. Math concepts are introduced quickly, and there is no time to fall behind.

CHAPTER 8

STRATEGIES FOR READING

"The more that you read the more things you will know. The more you learn the more places you'll go!"
—Dr. Seuss

I have a strong passion for teaching reading. Reading is an important skill for many content areas. Reading comprehension is needed to understand math word problems and science and social studies texts. Reading is a core skill that your child will need to be successful in life. In this chapter, we will share some key strategies you can use at home to support your child as they work virtually. Each tip will provide your child with the necessary practice they will need to sharpen their reading skills so that they can grow to be fluent readers.

Why Is Reading Important?

As noted, reading spans all content areas. Your child will be reading to learn once they get into the third grade. That is why early literacy is so important. Ensuring your child can read fluently is the main goal in primary grades. Once they get into third grade and beyond, the focus shifts to ensuring students can comprehend complex texts in order to evaluate, synthesize, and absorb information. We will begin the chapter with the pre-reading skills that primary children will need. We will then move on to phonics, after which our focus will turn to fluency and comprehension strategies.

Pre-K Reading

Whether or not your pre-K child is engaged in any sort of formal learning, you will want to start them on the path to literacy. Almost every parent does this instinctively by reading stories to their children at bedtime or at other times throughout the day. And which parent doesn't begin to recite the alphabet song to their child?

Reading Aloud

Reading aloud is the single most important activity that you can do on a daily basis to help your pre-K child build the pre-literacy skills that will enable them to quickly pick up on reading. Reading aloud builds a love for reading. Children who are read to are more likely to enjoy books and seek to read them on their own. Reading aloud also enables children to hear the structure of stories, which will help them with comprehension. By listening to stories, they begin to understand that stories have characters, and that the structure of a story has a beginning, a middle, and an end. It also helps to build their vocabulary as they read about different characters and topics. Reading aloud helps students become better writers. The more they are exposed to quality books, the better they get at writing their own stories. Finally, reading aloud helps you bond with your child as you share a very special time to enjoy the written word.

You may notice that your child wants you to read their favorite stories again and again. This is an excellent practice, as it allows your child to build their vocabulary and understanding of text structures, including the way text is organized. Chapters, paragraphs, tables of contents, and appendixes, to name a few, are all part of text structures. Depending on the type of text being read, you will encounter different text structures. The more familiar your child is with how nonfiction and fiction are structured, the better they will comprehend.

Don't be surprised when they memorize the words and recite the book aloud to you. This is another great precursor to reading. As students are reciting the text, they are gaining skills in fluency. In the Appendix, you'll find a list of great books to read aloud to your child.

Here is a structure you can use when reading stories aloud with your child.

◇◇◇◇◇◇

READING STORIES ALOUD

Step 1. Read the title of the book. Talk about what the title may signify about what the book is going to be about. (This helps kids learn the importance of thinking about what they are about to read, which increases comprehension.)

Step 2. Look at the picture on the cover of the book and talk about what you see. What might it reveal about what is to come in the book? Some books have pictures of the main characters or of an important aspect of the setting. Talk about what you see and why you think the author and/or illustrator picked this picture to be depicted on the front cover.

Step 3. Go on a "picture walk," which means flipping through the pages of the book and looking at the illustrations. Talk about what you see in the pictures. Your child may mention that they see an animal or a character. Let them talk about what sticks out to them as you look through the book. If there are important characters or events, you can talk about the fact that it looks like something important is happening here, or say, "This character looks excited and I wonder why." All of these comments will depend on what you are viewing in the book.

Step 4. Begin reading the story. Be sure to read with expression and interest, as this will instill more enjoyment in the story reading for your child.

Step 5. As you read aloud, have your child recite with you any text that is repeated. Some books have a pattern and repeat words from page to page. If this is the case, have you child engage with the text by reciting with you.

Step 6. Ask questions like, "What do you think will happen next?" as you come to sections of the book that have a change in setting or an important event coming up. This will help your child understand that we think about what we are reading and anticipate what is going to happen next.

Step 7. After you finish the book, ask your child questions about the text. Some good questions include: "What happened at the beginning of the story?" "What happened at the end of the story?" "What did you like best about the story?" "What did you like least about the story?"

Step 8. After reading the story, summarize what happened in the story. This will help you child pull together the storyline, which helps with comprehension.

◇◇◇◇◇◇

ABCs

Pre-K children should begin to learn the letters of the alphabet. Most parents start by having their kids sing or recite the alphabet song. The alphabet song is catchy and easy to memorize. This is a great way to introduce the letters to pre-K children and to teach them to pronounce the letter names. I would also suggest writing the letters of the alphabet on index cards to show to your child as you sing the alphabet song. Parents often ask if they should teach uppercase (capitals) or lowercase letters of the alphabet. Since your child will more often see lowercase in books, magazines, etc., it is important they can recognize the lowercase alphabet letters, though I suggest teaching both lower- and uppercase letters at the same time. Use the wording: "This is a capital A and this is a lowercase a" to distinguish between them.

Alphabet Books

You can read alphabet books to your child to help them learn the letters. There are so many cute alphabet books to choose from; you'll find them on just about any subject. The key is to find alphabet books that your child will find interesting. If your child likes animals, find an alphabet book on animals. Choose alphabet book topics that are of high interest so your child will be learning and having fun at the same time. There are so many diverse alphabet books out there on everything from sports to ballet. You will have so much fun finding alphabet books to match your child's interests.

Next, you want to start introducing your child to the letters in their name. Do this by talking about the letters in their name and showing them what the letter symbols look like.

Here is an example of how to teach you pre-K child the letters in their name.

◇◇◇◇◇◇

LEARN THE LETTERS IN YOUR NAME

Step 1: Make letter cards using index cards or any other type of paper with only the letters in your child's name. The letters should be written in marker and cut into strips so they can be easily manipulated to spell your child's name. The first letter of the name should be a capital letter, and the remaining letters should be lowercase.

Step 2: Tell your child you are going to be teaching them the letters in their name.

Step 3: Say the following: "Mary, your name is spelled M-A-R-Y. The first letter in your name is M—this is an M." Show the M card. Next, show the a card and say, "The second letter in your name is a. This is an a." Show the letter a card. Continue until you finish with the letters in your child's name.

Step 4: Take the letter cards of your child's name and put them in order on a flat surface. Go back over the letters and start teaching your child to say the letters in their name.

With practice, they will soon be able to recognize the letters in their name and spell their name.

◇◇◇

The reason we are advocating for working with the letters in your child's name is that the letter-symbol relationship plays a big role in familiarizing your child with the letters of the alphabet. The more that students can see the letters and associate them with an object, the more quickly they will learn the alphabet.

K–1 Reading

Kindergarten and first grade are the most important levels for learning to read. It is during these pivotal years that students learn the foundational skills they will need to be able to break the reading code. Learning to read is such an important milestone for children. It brings such a feeling of independence and joy. Reading requires that students can identify the letter and the sound, and blend those sounds together to read a word. This is a complex process that is taught systematically using phonics instruction.

In this section, we will share top tips to use at home that will support your kindergarteners and first graders with acquiring the important preliteracy and literacy skills they will need to build their reading abilities.

Print Concepts

Print concepts refer to book handling and word recognition skills that your child will need to master to prepare to become a reader. You can model these strategies when reading aloud to your child. Start by showing your child how you hold a book and how we track words from left to right when we read. These book-handling skills are not intrinsically known by children who are learning to read. It is important to explicitly show your child how to hold a book. Have you ever seen a child holding a book upside down or starting to look at a book from the back page? These are behaviors that show you the child does not have a clear understanding of print concepts. Learning print concepts when they are being taught virtually is very difficult; thus, taking the time to work on these skills at home with your child is critical.

As with all the strategies in this chapter, print concepts should be reinforced in a natural setting. When you are reading a bedtime story to your child, you can casually talk about how to hold the book properly, and as you read, point to the words and talk about how we read from left to right. These casual conversations go a long way in teaching young children reading behaviors.

Letter Names

Learning the names of the letters of the alphabet, which we began with pre-school children, is necessary for your kindergarten student to master. The sooner that they can recognize the letters, the sooner they can begin to associate them with their letter sound. As noted, learning to read is a very precise science that is amazing. Once kids break the code of reading, it is so exciting for everyone involved, including the teacher, but especially for the child. The look on their face when they are able to read on their own is priceless.

To assist your child with letter recognition, immerse them with books on the letters of the alphabet, and you can also lead them to practice writing the letters of the alphabet. As they are tracing the letters, ask them to say the letter names. Research has found that when we add movement to learning, kids pick up on the learning at faster rates.

Following is a structure you can use to help with letter naming.

◇◇◇◇◇◇
LETTER-NAMING STRATEGY

Materials needed:
- Printed dotted alphabet letters sheet
- Pencil

Step 1. Print out a page with the letters of the alphabet and dotted lines so your child can trace the letters. (There are many free online websites that have printable alphabet letters. See the Appendix for some ideas.)

Step 2: Tell your child that you are going to practice writing and saying the letters of the alphabet.

Step 3: Model for your child by going through one of the practice sheets. As you trace each letter, say the name of the letter.

Step 4. Do a few of the letters together with your child. You may need to trace a couple of letters with them by holding the pencil together. Note: Do not emphasize letter formation during this exercise. The focus is on having your child name the letters of the alphabet.

Step 5: Continue until you complete the template paper.

Step 6. Ask your child to go back over the sheet. Have them point to the letters and say the letter names.

Continue with this activity until your child can do it independently. It may take a few weeks or months for your child to master all of the letters.

◇◇◇◇

Another strategy to promote letter recognition is to use flash cards to drill your child on the letters of the alphabet. You can print alphabet cards or purchase them at a bookstore, and some department stores sell them. Simply go through the alphabet cards in random order and quiz your child on letter recognition. For this exercise, I prefer cards that only show the letters of the alphabet. Some cards come with pictures on them. I would stay away from those for teaching letter recognition because you want the focus to be on the letters and not the pictures on the cards. When you do the flash card drill, you will show your child the card and ask them to name the letter. If they say the incorrect letter name, tell them the correct letter name and put it back into the pile to be called again.

Learning the names of the letters is an important part of early literacy. When your child can quickly name the letters, they will be more readily able to begin to learn the sounds associated with the letters. Continue to work on this skill with your child until they've mastered it. It is also a good idea to review the letter names once your child can name them all. This will ensure the letter names stay fresh in their memory.

Letter Sounds

Another key reading skill is to know the letter sounds. This skill is essential to becoming a reader. You can support this at home by practicing the sounds of the letters with your child. If you are not sure how to pronounce some of the sounds, there are numerous videos online that teach the letter sounds. You can watch a video with your child and go over the sounds together.

You can also go through the letter cards and say the letter sounds along with your child. To test them on their knowledge, you can have your child say the letter sounds to you independently. If they miss a sound, say the sound for them and put the card back into the pile so they can try it again.

Learning letter sounds takes time. Children may grasp certain letter sounds more quickly than others. It takes patience and perseverance to learn all of them. The key is to keep going over them with your child. In time, they will memorize them all. Just don't give up, and keep practicing.

Another drill is to sing songs that teach the letter sounds. Again, there are so many excellent letter-sound videos that you can watch online. Choose one that interests your child and learn the song together. I have found that children learn their letter sounds quickly when they have a song to associate them with.

In the next section, we will talk about phonics. In order for your child to be successful in their phonics instruction, they will need to know their letter sounds. Ensure you are continuing to review these so that your child can easily use them to sound out words when they are learning to read.

Phonics

Phonics will be the main focus of your child's reading instruction in kindergarten and first grade. To support their phonics instruction at home, you can read books with your child that have the phonics pattern that the teacher is covering. Find out what the phonics focus is for the week and look for books that are on the same phonics pattern. If they're working on, for example, a short a or the consonant c, find books with those sounds and ask your child to identify them. The idea is to make it playful. As your child progresses into first grade, they will learn blends, such as ar or ir. Finding books with words that contain the ir phonic, like fir or girl, are great ways to make learning the phonics skill accessible and practical.

Another idea to help your child with phonics at home is for them to read words to you using their phonics knowledge. For example, help your child read CVC words—words with a consonant, vowel, consonant. Examples are the words cat and hat. Tell them that the beginning consonant in the word cat is the letter

c. The vowel is *a*, and the ending consonant is *t*. Students begin reading CVC words in kindergarten as they are learning the consonant sounds. It will be important to talk with your child's teacher to find out the phonics skills they are working on so you can have your child practice reading those words at home.

You can make index cards that show the letters of the alphabet. Cut the cards into thirds and write one letter on each strip. Put the letters in order to spell the word, and ask your child to read them by sounding out each letter and blending them together.

Check with your child's teacher to find out what blending routine they use. Some teachers have kids slide the sounds using their arms. That is when the child uses their arm as a visual to represent each letter sound. For example, with the word "cat," students would slide their hand from the top to bottom of their arms and say the beginning c, middle a, and ending *t* sounds to read the word "cat." Others may have them use their fingers to point to the letters and then slide them together to read them. For instance, if the letters to the word "cat" were on a page, the students would point to the letter c and say "c;" they would then point to the a and say "a"; finally, they would point to the *t* and say "t." They would then slide their finger under the word "cat" and read it. There is no right or wrong way to teach children to blend—to maintain consistency, check with your child's teacher so you are supporting them in the blending routines they are using at school.

There are some great online resources for teaching phonics that you can use to support your child, but don't forget the importance of having your child work with physical books and tools as they are learning to read. Some of my favorite online sources for phonics are kizphonics.com, abcmouse.com, and phonicsbloom.com Your child's teacher may have some other websites or applications they recommend.

There is a strong connection between learning to read and tactile or physical actions. Allowing your child to use objects like beans or blocks to represent letters as they are learning to blend words is a good strategy. The movement of the items as they say each letter sound is a great way to help kids internalize the process of reading.

Final Tips on Phonics

We have shared some key strategies you can use to support your child as they are learning phonics. The main takeaway is to make sure you are in contact with your child's teacher so you can ensure you are supporting the phonics skills that are being taught in class. If your child does not master a letter, let the teacher know so they can provide you with support. Phonics is the doorway to reading. It is imperative that your child stays up on their phonics instruction so they can become fluent readers.

Comprehension

Reading is not just about reading words, but comprehending what those words are saying. Comprehension is the purpose for reading. We read to understand messages. Your kindergartener or first-grader can practice comprehension skills at home by talking to you about the stories that you read together. A simple routine is to ask your child to tell you what is happening in the story while you both read. We know that a lot of brainpower goes into decoding or reading words, but you don't want your child to forget the main purpose for reading. Taking the time to read together for fun is essential for building comprehension. As you read, here are some comprehension questions you can ask:

- What is this story mainly about?

- Who are the characters?

- What is happening now in the story?

- How do you think the characters feel?

- What do you think is going to happen next?

This is just a small selection of sample questions that will keep your child thinking as you're reading together. We talked about phonics in the previous section. Phonics material is not known for having storylines that promote comprehension lessons. That is why it is important to continue to read aloud with your child daily and ask these types of questions. This will allow them to understand the main purpose of reading, which is to comprehend information.

Second- and-Third Grade Reading

Students in the second and third grade begin to build on the basic reading skills (phonics, print concepts, and comprehension) they have obtained in kindergarten and first grade. The concepts quickly escalate, especially in third grade, when the approach begins to shift from learning to read to reading to learn. This means that the teacher will not spend as much time on phonics skills but will begin to focus more on comprehension skills, as children begin to read more complex texts. It is very easy for children to fall behind in third grade if they do not have the basics of reading under their belt. That is why we emphasized early literacy and basic phonics skills in kindergarten and first grade. In this section, we will provide tips for you to support your child as they move into more complex reading tasks.

Phonics

Your child will be working on more complex phonics skills in the second and third grade. By the end of first grade, their reading should become more fluent, and in second grade, they will begin to focus on more difficult phonics patterns like digraphs and double consonants. Digraphs are words like *stick* and *brick*, which have the *ck* sound—two successive letters that create a single sound. Double-consonant words include *toss* and *boss*, with the doubles at the end of the word. Again, check with your child's teacher to ensure you know what phonics skill they are focusing on so you know what to reinforce at home. During your phonics reinforcement, you want to practice the skills with your child, and again find books that have the phonics pattern they are focusing on.

You can also ask your child to write words with the phonics pattern and then read them back to you. As your child reads and writes the words, they are getting more familiar with the phonics pattern, which will cause them to retain the new learning.

REVIEWING PRIOR PHONICS SKILLS

If your child has a deficit or areas of phonics that they are still working on, take some time to review with them. This can include going over the letter sounds and encouraging your child to practice reading and writing words with the given phonics pattern. You can get this information by asking your child's teacher if there are any areas in phonics that your child needs support in. You can follow the same routine we shared in the kindergarten and first-grade section. The key is to keep practicing the skills until your child can read and write them without support.

If you find that your child is really struggling with a particular phonics skill, ask the teacher what type of support they can provide at the school. Again, it is pivotal that your child master this before third grade, where the focus will shift more on reading to learn instead of learning to read.

Spelling

Spelling practice can be an effective way to review phonics patterns. Create spelling lists and request that your child study the words before their weekly spelling test, which the school creates and administers. If your child does not have weekly spelling tests, you can create your own spelling tests to administer to your child. Make the spelling lists uniform and ensure that they are on a particular phonics pattern. If you are creating a spelling list with *ck* words, only use words with *ck* in them on the list, such as *chick, stick, flick,* and so on.

I suggest keeping your spelling list to five or ten words. Your goal is to help your child practice the phonics pattern, and you do not want to overwhelm them with a long, exhaustive list.

◇◇◇◇◇◇

SPELLING PRACTICE ACTIVITIES

To practice the spelling in context, instruct your child to write sentences using the spelling words, and then ask them to read the sentences back to you. This is an excellent way to build a story around the words, which will make them easier to remember.

Your child can use Play-Doh or different colored markers and pens to spell their words. This is a way to bring creativity into the spelling process. If your child likes nature, they can use leaves to spell out their words. This would look like using the leaves to spell out words that are then pasted or glued to paper. You can make it into a fun art project by having them paste the leaves on paper in a decorative way. The idea is to make learning fun.

◇◇◇◇

Comprehension

The purpose of reading is to comprehend what is written. As students move into second grade, the expectations for comprehending text increase, and by third grade, the majority of the standards focus on comprehension. There are several ways to support this skill at home. Students may struggle with understanding how to find information in the text. This is especially more difficult when students are reading text from online sources on the computer screen. If you are finding that your child is having trouble reading electronic text, ask your child's teacher if they can send paper copies home, or possibly you can download and print documents at home. We know that most state assessments are now taken online. This shift typically happens in third grade. Paper documents are a good scaffold for young readers in second grade, but once children enter third grade, you'll want to taper off from paper support and begin to find ways for your child to read electronic text.

Comprehension Tips

Asking and answering questions about the stories being read is a top way to support comprehension. On page 91, we listed some questions to ask when reading with your child. Following are some comprehension questions related to comprehension that are appropriate for second and third graders.

- Who is/are the main character(s) in the story?
- What is the conflict in the story?
- What information in the text supports your idea?
- What would you do if you were in the same situation as the character?

Fourth- and Fifth-Grade Reading

The level of text complexity increases greatly in fourth and fifth grades. At these grade levels, students will be reading multiple accounts of stories and texts and are expected to find similarities and differences in the accounts. Now, the teaching of reading itself is not the focus, as the standards require students to read texts as if they are detectives pulling out details to support their claims. Following are some tips to help your child with text complexity and comprehension.

Text Complexity

As your child enters fourth grade, you will notice that the texts they read become increasingly more complex. This includes both the subject matter and the reading levels. This again reiterates our focus in the earlier grades on ensuring our students have a good grasp of reading so they can spend their time focused on understanding the complex nature of the texts and not trying to figure out how to read the words on the page or screen.

To support your child with reading complex texts, ensure you are providing them with time to practice reading every day. Make it a habit for your child to read for at least thirty minutes per day. The texts they read should be at their reading level. If your child struggles with the words, you can have them write the problematic words and you can help them pronounce those words.

Another idea is to let them listen to recorded books as they follow along with their own copy of the text. This allows them to hear the correct pronunciation and also supports fluency, which we will talk about next.

> **Success Tip:** A very important measure is to find out your child's reading level. You can get this from your child's teacher. This will allow you to pick books at their grade level to support them at home.

Fluency

Fluency refers to the ability to read texts without stopping to decipher words, which hinders comprehension. Think of a news anchor who reads the news in a conversational manner that sounds like natural language. This is how we want our students to read. Fluency is one of the measures we use to predict comprehension. When you read in a conversational flow, you are better able to remember what you are reading. If your reading is choppy and you continue to have to stop and sound out words, your comprehension decreases.

Ask your child to read a passage that is on their grade level aloud to you and note how their reading sounds. Use the following chart to help you.

FLUENCY ASSESSMENT

Reading sounds like a conversation.	■ YES ■ NO
Reading is choppy—stops two to five times to sound out words.	■ YES ■ NO
Reading has expression.	■ YES ■ NO
Pays attention to the punctuation, stops at periods, and vocalizes explanation marks.	■ YES ■ NO

Look at the responses to the Fluency Assessment. If your child's reading sounds like a conversation, compliment them on their fluency. Let them know this is what fluent readers sound like.

If your child's reading is choppy, look at the words they have missed and go over them. Continue to practice fluent reading.

If your child reads with expression, meaning they sound animated and/or somber depending on the text, let them know that this is what fluent readers sound like and they should continue with this practice.

If your child is not paying attention to punctuation, remind them to slow down and look at the punctuation so they are reading the text the way the author intended.

Comprehension

Comprehending text in fourth and fifth grade involves looking for clues in the written material to come up with supported conclusions. Students are required to base their conclusions not on personal opinion, but on facts and inferences pulled from the text that they are reading. Here are some ways to support these skills.

Searching for Evidence

Fourth and fifth graders need to search the text to find evidence that will support what they believe the material conveys. They may have to share what the author says that shows their support or opposition to a given topic or issue. You can facilitate this by having your child share with you what the author's opinion is on a given topic. You can find news stories or books around the house. If the text is too difficult for your child to read, you can read it aloud together. This purpose of this activity is not reading fluency, but to practice searching for evidence in the text. Here is an example:

> **Text:** Mr. and Mrs. Jack have an acre of land that they want to use to help reduce the effects of air pollution in their area. Mrs. Jack has proposed that she and her husband plant trees in the backyard to help reduce the greenhouse effect. Mr. Jack agrees, so they set out to their local garden nursery to pick trees.

> **Question:** What evidence can you cite from the text to show that Mrs. and Mr. Jack support the environment?

Answer: Student can cite the fact that Mrs. Jack wants to plant trees in her backyard and Mr. Jack agrees, so they go to find trees at their local garden nursery.

This is a simple example of how students are asked to support their answers with specific evidence from the text. Find articles, stories, and material that you and your child find interesting, and make up questions like this so your child can get used to pulling information from the text to answer questions.

Middle School Reading

As students enter middle school, they will encounter more sophisticated reading material with increasingly complex topics. The vocabulary they are reading will become more difficult. With this comes an important focus on reading carefully and ensuring they are paying attention to the words in the written text. During middle school, my tip is to have your kids slow down when they are reading and to take notes as they go through the text. This will allow them to hold on to their ideas so they can ensure they are understanding the content. Here are some tips to assist your child at home.

Comprehension

Children in middle school should be setting a purpose for their reading before they dive in. Before they start reading, talk to your child about looking at the questions that they are going to be required to answer after they finish the text. This will help them focus their attention on those key ideas and eliminate a lot of re-reading to find text evidence. This strategy can be helpful in all grade levels, but it becomes essential for middle school students. In grades six and seven, your child will be expected to read longer passages with a lot of dense material. By setting a clear purpose, they have a laser focus for their reading.

Inferences

The fiction that your child will be reading in middle school will have deeper themes and more flowery language. This will require that your child infer meaning, which involves looking at the words on the page or screen and reading beyond them. For example, a poem about flowers may really represent people and how we grow as we mature in age. This inferencing comes from reading the words and looking for their meaning based on the context of the text. You can support drawing inferences by asking your child to look for examples where the words on the page have more than a surface meaning. Good authors to read to work on inferencing include Kwame Alexander, Shel Silverstein, and Thanhha Lai.

Note-Taking

Taking notes when reading text to keep track of important facts, inferences, themes, etc., is a great strategy to reinforce with your child. Your child's teacher may have a specific note-taking system that is used in class. You can ask if they have one that you can reinforce at home. If they do not have a specific note-taking strategy, you can create your own. Note-taking can be as simple as getting a sheet of paper and folding it into four parts. You can label the four sections to relate to the areas that your child is focusing on finding. If your child is looking for inferences and themes, those would be two of the labels in the boxes.

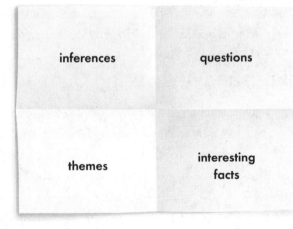

Diverse Texts

Ensure your child has access to diverse texts. Encouraging them to read fiction, nonfiction, articles, and biographies will help them build their vocabulary and comprehension skills. The more diverse readers they are, the easier it will be for them to respond to questions about different genres of works. We all have our favorite genre that we enjoy reading. I enjoy nonfiction, plays, and mysteries. Your child may enjoy real-life sports books and biographies. What we love, we gravitate to, so my bookshelves are filled with mysteries, plays, and nonfiction books. This is probably the case with your child. To diversify their reading habits, suggest that they explore genres they might not often lean toward. Pick up some poetry books or plays so they can have experience reading/comprehending those types of texts, if it's not what they normally favor. This will be especially important as they prepare to enter high school, where they will be introduced to different genres and will be expected to read and make sense of them.

High School Reading

In high school, all the reading skills come into play in diverse books with more mature themes and topics. Your child will also be reading texts from their science, social studies, and other content areas that will be at higher reading levels with very complex vocabulary. By this time, your child will be expected to read these texts independently with little to no support from the teacher. Here are some tips to help your child build this independence.

Asking and Answering Questions

A great way to help your child practice their comprehension strategies is to advise them to write questions that they think would be useful to teach the concepts of comparing, contrasting, and inferring. By writing questions and the related answers, your child will be working at a high level. We comprehend more when we teach others. After many years of experience with comparing, contrasting, and inferring, the next step is to write those questions themself. This allows your child to be a teacher of sorts. You can ask them to read passages and write questions for you to answer. I have done this exercise with my own child and it helped build his comprehension skills greatly.

Vocabulary

Increasing vocabulary is important for high school students. Again, the written material they will encounter will have some difficult words. A fun way to build your child's vocabulary is for them to learn a new word each day. We did this with a family member who was studying for the SATs. By practicing a vocabulary word each day, she was able to increase her scores on the SAT assessment. There are many online apps that send vocabulary words to your phone. Find an app that you would like to use to learn new words. There are some suggested apps in the Appendix. To demonstrate your child's knowledge of the new word, invite them to text you a sentence using a new word each day. It is a way to connect with your high school student, and it serves to help increase their vocabulary.

You can also encourage your child to make a vocabulary journal. This involves getting a blank notebook where they write new words that they learn. I kept one of these when I was in school. It allowed me to increase my vocabulary so I could articulate myself more eloquently, and I could use it in my writing. It also helped me tremendously with my comprehension of complex texts. I was an English literature major in college, and my years of keeping vocabulary journals came in very handy when I was reading Shakespeare and some of the other literary greats.

Closing Thoughts on Reading

This chapter has been filled with information to help you support your kindergarten through twelfth-grade child with practical strategies to use at home to support virtual reading instruction. Most of the tips involve low-tech suggestions to support reading. There are many online applications that can be used, and those are listed in the Appendix. I hope you can find a few strategies to assist you as you work with your child to ensure they are reading at or above their grade level.

CHAPTER 9

STRATEGIES FOR WRITING

"The secret of becoming a writer is to write, write, and keep on writing."

—Ken MacLeod

Why Is Writing Important?

Writing is a subject that students often find challenging. This is because a lot of schools do not offer specific writing programs that teach students the step-by-step process to fully develop their writing skills. It takes years to grow into a proficient writer. Without proper practice and skill building, students can find writing tasking. Numerous families share that writing is an area of concern in the virtual learning space.

The steps to proficient writing begin with young children scribbling on paper and drawing stick figures. This early process grows into students spelling words phonetically and matching the pictures that they draw to the words on the page. As they move up in the grade levels, their ability to choose the right words to convey the meaning and tone that they want in their writing becomes more fine-tuned. And when they enter junior and senior year of high school, they must master the skill of research writing, where they learn to accurately quote sources to support their ideas.

When I was a teacher, I spent a lot of time imparting the craft of writing to my students. Writing has always been a passion of mine, as I understand how important it is to write in a clear manner in order to communicate. Almost every job requires you to do some sort of writing to provide information to others. This may be via email, or perhaps you need to submit written status reports, electronic sales reports, work orders—maybe you need to evaluate people in your department, write memos, or assess products or strategies. This list is very diverse. Writing is a life skill that must be cultivated in children.

I enjoy watching students put their thoughts on paper and seeing their satisfaction when their writing is published and shared with others. In this chapter, we will look at some strategies that you can adopt to support your child's writing instruction at home. Just as we emphasized the importance of reading with your child daily, I also encourage writing with them—if not daily then weekly, at a minimum, to foster these important skills.

Writing Matters

Writing is, in my opinion, the single most important subject that students need to master in order to be truly literate individuals. You cannot write if you cannot read, so there is a strong connection between reading and writing. We read written words; thus, writing is how we put our ideas on paper so they can be shared with others. As noted above, writing is important for our jobs. Writing is also important when your child enters college. Most college courses require essays as a means of assessing student understanding of content. In this chapter, we will take you through the process of writing as it starts in pre-K and progresses to high school.

Pre-K Writing

Your pre-K child will benefit from being offered opportunities to practice writing. Make writing a part of your normal routine. To begin with, make sure that you have writing utensils—pencil and paper are a good start for this age. Also, make sure that markers and/or crayons are readily available in the home. Keep all the writing tools in a centralized place for quick access.

Early writing for pre-K students should be a natural process of exploration. Children at this age level are exploring the world around them. Writing is often an exciting activity for them. If your child seems to have little or no interest in exploring writing, be patient and offer other writing tools. Maybe your child prefers writing with a crayon or perhaps with markers. Keep offering choices until you find their preferred writing medium.

In this section, we will discuss some things you can do at home to support your pre-K writers.

Get a Grip

Begin teaching your child to grip their writing utensils appropriately. The correct way to hold a writing utensil is to use the thumb and index finger to pinch the pencil. The middle finger will rest underneath the pencil, and the ring finger and pinky are tucked away (see the illustration).

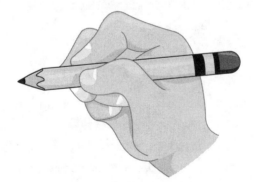

This is the correct way for your child to hold a pencil. Notice the position of the fingers: thumb and index finger grip the pencil, which rests on the middle finger.

There are also tools you can purchase online or at an educational supply store that teach your children to hold their writing utensils properly. Continue to practice holding the writing utensil correctly until it registers in your child's muscle memory.

Pencil grip is a developmental process. Your child may continue to need support in this as they enter kindergarten.

Scribble Writing

Scribble writing is an important part of learning to write for pre-k students. We can see so much in their scribbles. By allowing your child to explore writing by scribbling, they learn that words are written on a page to communicate, they get to express their ideas and feelings, and scribbling offers them the opportunity to build their gross motor skills.

Encourage your child to write/scribble and ensure you do not criticize their efforts. They are learning, and we are looking for effort and not perfection at this point.

Finger Painting

Another way to practice writing is to call upon your child's artistic side by using finger paints. This is an awesome way to build fine motor skills, and it's a lot of fun. Children can use their fingers to trace letters or to draw picture stories. You can model this by sharing pictures from storybooks and letting your child re-create their own masterpiece.

Chalk Writing

Sometimes the medium your child uses can encourage them to want to write more. Some children enjoy using sidewalk chalk to write messages, and this encourages them to practice writing. Ensure that you praise their efforts. During the pre-K years, students need a lot of encouragement and support as they are developing their fine motor skills and their hand and eye coordination as they are learning to write.

K–1 Writing

As mentioned, writing is one of the most important skills your child will need to master to be successful throughout their lives. We use writing each day to communicate with others. We write memos and emails to our colleagues to express ideas on a daily basis. Writing connects your child with reading. We read words that are written messages. It's important to take the time to reinforce writing skills. Many schools find that the time to teach writing is often cut short due to so many other concepts that need to be covered. I again want to emphasize the importance of focusing on writing support as it is, in my opinion, the single most critical skill your child will use for a lifetime. The skills they learn in kindergarten and first grade are pivotal so that children are ready for the more complex writing tasks they will encounter as they move up in the grade levels. In this section, we will discuss ways to promote writing proficiency by modeling writing, practicing handwriting, and writing for fun, to name a few. These strategies are easily implemented and will support your student as they grow on their writing journey.

Modeled Writing

As students are beginning to learn how to write, it is important that they see models of writing so they have examples of what good writing looks like. If you are able to watch your child's teacher conduct a writing lesson virtually, you may note that they are sharing their writing and talking through the process of how they put the words on the page. You may hear the teacher speaking as if they are talking to themselves as they are deciding where to add a capital letter or how to sound out a word. You may see them projecting their work via a smart camera or writing on a large piece of chart paper. This is an important teaching strategy called "modeled writing."

This modeling is how we introduce writing to pre-K and kindergarten students. You can do the same modeling with your child to reinforce early writing skills. Start by getting a piece of paper and having your child watch you write a message. As you are writing, talk about the process you are using to write your message. For example, talk about using capital letters at the beginning of the sentence and how you use periods at the end of your thought. Get your child involved by asking them to help you with the beginning sounds of words. Ask them which letter the word *cat* begins with. Ask them what sound is at the end of the word *dogs*. The trick is to be animated and to make your thinking visible to your child as you decide what to put on the page. This may be a bit difficult at first. As a fluent writer you know intrinsically how to put your thoughts on paper. This skill has to be modeled and taught to children just as we have to model and teach them to read. Give modeled writing a try, as it is a sure way to build writing proficiency for your primary school student.

Handwriting

Your child may still be working on building their fine motor skills. In the previous section, we shared some strategies to use to build fine motor skills. Use any of those with your child as they fine-tune their motor skills. Remember, with practice, their dexterity will improve. These muscles have to be built up, and this only happens with time and practice.

As detailed in Chapter Eight, one great way to help build handwriting is for your child to trace the letters of the alphabet so they can learn their proper formation. Be sure to model for your child how to write the letters. For instance, if you notice that your child is starting at the bottom of the line to write the letter *h*, model for them that we start at the top and work down. There are many online tools and videos that show proper letter formation. Look into these so you can have the right language to use as you model writing the letters with your child.

Writing Your Child's Name

There is nothing more important than our names to identify ourselves. Ensuring your child can write their first and last name without hesitation is a key skill you want to work on. Children are so proud when they can first write their names. To reinforce this, have your child practice writing their name on a daily basis. This should be part of your routine before you do any other schoolwork. You can make dots for your child to trace to write their name, or you can download an online program that you can use to print out your child's name with dots. In the Appendix at the end of the book, I share several free online websites that provide dotted fonts that you can use. These can also be used to practice writing letters of the alphabet.

Letter formation can be challenging for students. They are learning to write letters for the first time and to use a writing instrument. When I taught first grade it took sometimes half a year to break kids from the habit of forming letters incorrectly. When we write, it gets into our muscle memory, which can take some time to correct. That is why it is important to model the proper way to form letters so your child practices writing them the correct way. There are many online videos that you can watch that show proper letter formation for you to follow. It would be worth the effort to look at some of the videos to freshen your memory. Most of us write in cursive handwriting and by typing these days, so print writing may not be something you practice often.

Early Writing

As students are learning to put their ideas on paper, be sure to promote drawing pictures to support what they are writing. Picture drawing is an important part of early writing. These pictures relay the fine details that reinforce good writing. Think of all the storybooks that we read to children. They are filled with vivid pictures to support the words on the page.

Ask your child to draw pictures to match what they are writing about. Be sure that they understand that everything they draw should also be written about. For instance, if they draw a bluebird, they should include something written in their story about a blue bird. This is something to include during your modeled writing time.

Help Your Child Spell Correctly

Many parents contact me because their children are not spelling words correctly in their writing. Children in kindergarten and first grade are what we call "phonetic spellers." They use the sounds that they are learning and put them on paper to represent their ideas. It is common for a child to write cat as ct or mom as mmm. This is part of the developmental process of learning to write, which is very complex, as is learning to read. Children make tremendous gains in their writing skills over the school year. It may amaze you when you compare where your child is when they begin kindergarten with how much they've advanced by the end of the school year. The same is true for the growth in their writing skills in first grade. To ensure your child is making adequate progress in writing, I suggest checking in with your child's teacher at each parent-teacher conference to inquire about their writing development. Ask questions and share any relevant samples of writing that you may have at home. This is a great way to make sure your child is on track so you and the teacher can make any adjustments as needed.

Story Writing

The goal of writing is to convey our stories and messages in written format. To reinforce this connection, continue reading aloud with your child. As you do that, bring attention to the written page. Talk about how the words have spaces between them and how the author uses pictures to convey meaning. Look at the punctuation marks and denote how they change the way you read the text.

A fun way to introduce story writing to your child is to invite them to write a tale that mimics one of their favorite bedtime stories. Pick one that has a familiar pattern like *Brown Bear, Brown Bear, What Do You See?* by Bill Martin Jr., or any of Eric Carle's stories. The familiar pattern can easily be replicated in your child's own rendition of the story. Make sure to draw bright and colorful pictures to represent the words on the page. This activity can be partly a writing exercise and partly an art project. Activities like this help develop a love for writing in children.

Grammar

We have emphasized modeling for your child proper capitalization and looking at and using ending punctuation. In kindergarten and first grade, grammar consists of learning about nouns and verbs and learning to use capital letters and ending punctuation such as periods, questions marks, and exclamation points. In the earlier section, we mentioned how you can use them in your modeled writing and show them to your child during shared readings. To teach them more explicitly, you can talk about nouns and verbs in relation to the real world. For example, you can discuss the fact that a *dog* is a noun and a *bird* is noun, and that *running* is a verb and *singing* is a verb. The idea is to talk about the word's part of speech when you are interacting with your child naturally. As your child begins to become more familiar with nouns and verbs, ask them to tell you which items in your kitchen are nouns. When you are watching television, ask your child to tell you which verbs they see happening on the show.

Another activity is to divide a sheet of paper in the middle. Ask your child to write or draw pictures of nouns on the left and verbs on the right. Go over the list and discuss the items. Correct any misconceptions and praise your child for all correct answers.

Here is an example:

NOUNS	VERBS
Dog	Run
Lady	Walk

Adjectives

Adjectives are another grammar concept to focus on with your child. Adjectives are words used to describe things. A fun activity to do with adjectives is to find pictures in magazines and ask your child to describe the pictures using adjectives. For instance, if you are looking at a picture of a cloud, your child can use the adjectives *big*, *fluffy*, *white*, and *soft* to describe the cloud.

You can make this into an art project by cutting out the picture, gluing it to a larger piece of paper, and asking your child to label it with adjective words.

Ensure that you check with your child's teacher to find out which grammar concepts are being focused on at the time. Using this information, find ways to support these word concepts at home using the tips I have shared.

Spelling and Sight Words

Before we end our discussion on kindergarten and first-grade writing, I wanted to touch on the topic of spelling and sight words. Sight words are words that children should not have to decode using phonics. As its name signifies, "sight words" should be able to be read on sight quickly without thinking. The idea of sight words are words that your child will recognize in print and read without any prompting.

Words like *the* and *said* are considered sight words. Sight words can also include words that are frequently used like the color words (*red, blue, green,* etc.) and pronouns like *she* and *he*. Find out which sight words your child needs to master by the end of the school year. If you can get a list of them from the teacher, that would be preferred. Read the sight words with your child, and then ask them to write those words. This is a great way to practice the sight words, which you want them to memorize. To assess if your child has mastered a sight word, assure that they are able to read the word and write it independently and quickly without much effort.

As your child becomes more familiar with sight words, they should be able to spell them correctly. Instruct your child to write stories using the sight words. Check the spelling of the sight words and provide practice if they struggle with them.

Encourage the use of sight words in the writing that your child produces. By doing this, you are helping them with spelling and reading all in one setting.

Kindergarten to First-Grade Editing Checklist

❑ All of my sentences start with a capital letter.

❑ I use ending punctuation for all of my sentences.

❑ I use spaces between my words.

❑ My pictures match my text.

Second- and Third-Grade Writing

As children enter second and third grade, their writing skills build because they now have a few years of writing experience under their belts. As with reading, writing expectations gradually increase as students move through the grade levels. You will begin to see the biggest shift when your child reaches third grade. That is why it's important to practice writing exercises at home at least once a week. The strategies in this section can be used to practice essential skills that your second and third graders will need to become proficient independent writers.

Writing Prompts

Your child's teacher may provide writing prompts for them to expand on as a way to help them put their ideas on paper. Some common writing prompts include: "Write about your favorite way to spend the weekend," or "What did you do on your summer vacation?"

Teachers use writing prompts to help students frame a subject to expand on. There is nothing more frustrating than being told to write if you have no idea what to write about. When I was a beginning teacher, I noticed that when I did not give my students a specific writing prompt or a writing task, they often sat through the writing period staring at a blank page and not knowing where to start.

You can support your child at home by encouraging them to practice writing using prompts that you decide on. By providing these practice sessions, your child will develop confidence in their ability to compose text.

Here is a procedure to guide your child to write in response to a prompt.

WRITING PROMPTS PROCEDURE

STEP 1: Look at the list of writing prompts we provide a bit later in this chapter. Pick one that you think your child will enjoy writing about, or create your own prompt.

STEP 2: Gather writing paper and writing utensils for your child to use.

STEP 3: Find a quiet space where your child can focus. You may want to seat them in the space that you set up for virtual learning, or to mix things up, they can write in another part of the house. I like to encourage my child to write in different rooms of the house or even outdoors. Writing is a creative process and sometimes a change of scenery does the trick.

STEP 4: Let your child know that you will be giving them a topic to write about. Tell them that they should take their time when writing their response.

STEP 5: Read the chosen prompt to your child. Ask if they have any questions about the topic and respond to those questions.

STEP 6: Give your child twenty to thirty minutes to write on the topic. Let them know their time limit and set up a timer.

STEP 7: Let your child know that you just want them to do their best in their writing. Tell them that you will not be helping them during this process, and that they should not worry about spelling and grammar. Tell them this is just a fun writing prompt.

STEP 8: Set the timer and let your child begin.

STEP 9: When your child has five minutes left, let them know that time is almost up and that they might want to start wrapping up their writing.

STEP 10: When time is up, praise your child for their writing efforts. Ask them to read their story aloud to you.

> **Success Tip:** Some parents like to write alongside their child, using the same prompt. This is a great way to model writing practices with your child. If you have the time to do this, I would recommend it. Just as we model an importance for reading by reading books in front of our children, we do the same thing when we write with them.

Sample Writing Prompts

- What is your favorite way to spend the weekend?
- If you had $100, what would you buy and why?
- What do you like most about learning virtually?
- What do you like least about learning virtually?
- What is your favorite subject in school and why?
- What is your least favorite subject in school and why?
- Write about your favorite book or book character. Explain your choice.
- If you could go anywhere on vacation, where would you go?
- Which would you prefer to have—a pet fish or a pet cat? Explain your choice.
- Why should kids be allowed to stay up past midnight? Explain why.
- What job would you like to have when you grow up? Explain why.

Note that writing prompts should be used as a way to support the prompted writing your child is doing in school. I would suggest leading your child through prompted writing a couple of times per month as a check-in on their progress.

Writing prompts should be done in addition to the weekly writing assignments that your child is given. Teacher-provided assignments are more structured writing procedures, as opposed to the weekly writing you're guiding, which is for fun and less structured.

Grammar and Spelling

Grammar and spelling are continued areas of focus for support for second and third graders. In grammar, some of the key areas they will work on include plurals, possessives, and sight words.

Plurals

Students will learn about plural nouns. You can support this by showing your child what a plural represents. For example, show them a picture of a dog and then show them a picture of several dogs. Ask them to tell you verbally what the picture represents. To take it a step further, ask your child to cut out pictures of single animals or items and then pictures with more than one animal or item from magazines in your house. Once they have cut out their pictures, direct them to glue the pictures on blank sheets of paper and then to write what the pictures represent.

Here is a sample:

Insert a picture that looks as follows:

Dog   Dogs

Possessives

Your child will also be learning to write possessives. Reinforce possessive nouns by explaining that they show ownership and use an apostrophe. To illustrate, show your child an item in your house that belongs to you. Then write the words *mom's*, *dad's*, *grandma's*, etc., and put it on the item. Explain that the item, for instance, a mug, is *mom's*, *dad's*, *grandma's*, *John's*, or whichever possessive noun is appropriate.

Replicate the plurals example from above, and again ask your to child cut and paste pictures and label items.

Here is a sample:

Kierra's doll

Robert's book

Ask your child to continue to practice identifying plural and possessive nouns in the real world. This will make the learning more meaningful and bridge the connection between what they are learning virtually and what they experience around them.

Sight Words

Sight words continue to be an area of focus for your second- and third-grade students. Obtain a list of sight words from your child's teacher and follow the same procedure we shared in the kindergarten and first-grade section. Again, we want children to master these sight words, which means they can write and spell them independently with little to no effort.

> **Success Tip:** If your child has sight words from earlier grades that they have not mastered, continue to review them by giving your child time to practice writing those words and including them in their writing pieces.

Make a chart for your child to track their progress learning sight words. Use stickers to signify sight words that have been mastered. Children love to see their progress as they accomplish goals. Charts with stickers are very motivating for students. Stickers can be found at your local chain stores and most discount stores. Let your child pick the stickers that they like, to make earning them even more rewarding. And don't forget seasonal stickers for, say, Halloween, Thanksgiving, whatever your family may celebrate.

Opinion Writing

Your child will be asked to share their opinions in their writing, in other words, why they feel a particular way about a subject. In second and third grade, students may be asked to share their opinions about the actions of a character. Most of us are familiar with the story of Goldilocks and the three bears. The students may be asked to share how they feel about the actions of Goldilocks using evidence from the text to support their ideas.

An example would be if they wrote that they felt Goldilocks was selfish, because she went into the bears' house and ate all of baby bear's porridge, which did not belong to her.

Build on opinion writing by asking your child's opinion about stories that you read together or stories that you see on television. These conversations can build their understanding of how we support our opinions with information from the text or from the story. You can ask them to write about their opinions using evidence to again supplement opinion writing at home.

Nonfiction Writing and Research

Research writing is a style of writing that your child will encounter throughout their schooling. Knowing how to research a topic and writing about the findings will be the main form of writing that's expected as they get into middle school and high school. We begin learning how to write research papers in second and third grade. You can support research writing at home by inviting your child to look up things online and report the findings to you. For example, if you are considering buying a puppy, your child can do the research on the best breed of dog for your family and present their findings in writing to all of you.

Make researching fun and a natural part of how decisions are made in the home. This will enable your child to find research writing nonthreatening and turn it into a familiar practice, which will spill over into their school life.

I have included a list of topics that you might consider asking your child to research.

- Choosing a pet
- Best restaurant for a birthday party
- Family vacation spots
- Best skateboard, skates, bike, or similar
- Best places to go on field trips
- Most interesting foreign country or US state to visit
- Best types of plants for your yard, home, or apartment
- Most interesting streaming service to subscribe to
- What are the best ways to stay healthy and fit
- Best sports team of all time
- Most important inventions in the twentieth century
- Most influential women in history

Editing

The task of editing their work is an essential skill that students need to practice. You can support this by having your child review their writing whenever you work on a piece of writing together or they have a writing assignment for class.

Check with your child's teacher to see what editing process they use in school so you can supplement this at home. Most teachers have an editing checklist that they use. I have shared one below that may be appropriate for your child.

Second- and Third-Grade Editing Checklist

- ❏ All of my sentences start with a capital letter.
- ❏ I use ending punctuation for all of my sentences.
- ❏ I have checked to make sure my response answers the writing prompt of the assignment.
- ❏ I have checked my spelling.

Fourth- and Fifth-Grade Writing

Writing tasks continue to increase in difficulty as students move into fourth and fifth grades. In this section, we will look at strategies to support research writing and vocabulary.

Research Writing

We discussed research writing in the last section and noted how it becomes more of the focus of academic writing as students move through the grade levels. Fourth and fifth graders will be expected to write research papers that include more details and supporting documentation than in prior years.

To support this writing practice at home, look at the research topics that your child will be required to write about in class. You should be able to get this information from your child's teacher. Pick one of the topics and have your child write a sample paper at home with your support.

During this process, your role is to provide your child with time to practice their research-writing skills in a nonthreatening environment. As your child writes their paper, make sure they are paying close attention to the checklist their teacher provides or the sample checklist below:

Fourth- and Fifth-Grade Research Writing Checklist

- ❑ I have checked my punctuation.
- ❑ I have checked my spelling.
- ❑ I have checked to make sure my response answers the writing prompt of the assignment.
- ❑ I have reread my paper.

Introductions and Conclusions

Writing strong introductory and concluding paragraphs is a focus for fourth and fifth graders. An introduction should set up the reader for what is to come in the body of the essay, and the conclusion should provide the reader with a quick synopsis of what was written. In my experience, students need a lot of extra help understanding how to write solid introductory and concluding paragraphs. You can support these efforts at home by encouraging your child to read research papers with the purpose of paying attention to how the authors compose their introductions and conclusions. Your child's teacher should be able to provide you with some research papers that can serve as an example of what acceptable writing looks like. These are called "anchor papers." The purpose of anchor papers is to show students how writing is crafted on the page. When I was a teacher, I used them to help my students develop proficiency in their writing.

Just as we learn to be better readers by reading high-quality literature, we learn to be better writers by reading and studying quality writing.

Another way to help your children with nonfiction writing is to talk about the writing that you read together. If you are reading newspaper or online articles, talk about the choice of words that the author has used and the way they wrote about the subject. Discuss details of what you like about their writing, and what you might do differently. These casual conversations are pivotal for building your child's writing skills.

Supporting Details

Supporting details hold our writing together. They provide the specific information our readers need to know to understand our topics on a higher level. Helping your student find the most appropriate supporting details for a piece of writing involves understanding the purpose of supporting details—simply, they hold up the main idea. For example, if the main idea of the writing is about the Grand Canyon, the supporting details may include the terrain of the canyon, the climate of the canyon, and the indigenous people who call the canyon home.

The Three-Legged Stool

We often use the "three-legged stool" image to depict how supporting details hold up a main idea.

As you can see in the illustration, the main idea is the Grand Canyon, which is depicted as the seat of the stool. The three supporting details make up the legs of the stool.

We are using a three-legged stool because in most writing, we focus on three main ideas to support our main topic. If the teacher uses a different image, please go along with their recommendation.

Supporting Details Hunt

Go on a treasure hunt of sorts with your child to find the supporting details in a text. Find an article in a children's magazine or online and ask your child to find the supporting details that the author has included. Ask your child to underline or highlight them. Discuss the supporting details that were found and how they helped to bolster the main idea. This is a great way for your child to see how authors build their case in nonfiction and other published writing. Continue with this practice until your child is able to readily find the supporting details without your help.

Vocabulary

Students in fourth and fifth grade will be expected to use more academic vocabulary in their writing. They will be reading subjects such as science and social studies that have very distinct language. A way to help your child use this higher level of vocabulary and include it in their writing is to advise them to keep a vocabulary journal. This journal can be a simple three-ring notebook.

I suggest creating vocabulary sections for writing fiction and nonfiction. Your child should refer to their notebook when they are doing any sort of writing so they can include the words in their drafts.

Middle School Writing

Middle school requires that students write papers that are longer and have increased levels of rigor in how they are presented. The focus in middle school is mainly on research writing, and your child may be required to write about multiple subjects; for instance, they will have to turn in papers in their science and English classes. Middle school writers should be more independent, as they have had many years of writing experience to this point. This means that they may not be given as much school support with their writing tasks. This becomes more obvious when we are working in virtual models, where teacher-student interaction is not as frequent as it is in earlier grades. Therefore, you may need to offer more support at home, especially if you see that your child is not yet fully independent.

Research Writing

Guiding your child to read research writing is a great way to support the rigor expected in middle school writing. Find articles on subjects that your child has an interest in, and instruct them to read with the purpose of looking at how the author has composed their essay.

We find that children are better fiction writers because we spend so much time reading stories to them as they are growing up. We don't typically read non-fiction articles aloud to our children, so they often are not as skilled in writing this genre. Nonfiction writing also requires a lot of research, which students can find challenging. Fiction writing allows students to use their imagination, which can be a lot more enjoyable.

As we've noted, research writing becomes the focus of most writing tasks in middle school and beyond. Therefore, exposing your child to nonfiction articles and essays is a great way to build those skills.

Use the checklist below or the checklist that your child's school provides to help your child assess their research writing. Checklists are increasingly important as students move up the grade levels. They will help ensure your child is including all the necessary components of the writing task.

Research-Writing Checklist for Middle School

- ❑ I have checked my grammar and spelling.
- ❑ I have checked to make sure my response answers the writing prompt of the assignment.
- ❑ I have included high-quality references.
- ❑ I have reread my paper twice.

Grammar

The use of verbs is an important grammar focus for middle school students. Two main areas of middle school grammar are verb tense and irregular verbs. Let's briefly look at both areas.

Consistent Verb Tense

Many students struggle with maintaining consistent verb tense in a paragraph or sentence. For example, they may start the sentence in the past tense and then switch to present tense as the sentence progresses.

Verb Tense Example: Yesterday, Joyce drove her new car for the first time. She stops at every corner to make sure she is safe.

In this example, the sentence starts in the past tense and switches to present tense. This is not correct.

Share the above example with your child and ask them to look at a piece of their own writing to see if they are maintaining consistent verb tense.

Irregular Verbs

Irregular verbs are another area of focus for middle school students. Irregular verbs do not follow our typical pattern of adding ed or d to the end of verbs to signify past tense; the past tense of bust is busted and the past tense of rust is rusted, for instance. But irregular verbs need to be memorized because they are so nonstandard. Here are some examples of commonly used irregular verbs:

COMMON IRREGULAR VERBS

PRESENT TENSE	PAST TENSE
Awake	Awoke
Be	Was/Were
Begin	Began
Drink	Drank
Hide	Hid
Hold	Held
Know	Knew
Lie	Lied
Play	Played
Speak	Spoke
Write	Wrote

There are many lists available online of irregular verbs that would be beneficial for your child to study. You can suggest that they create a list of common irregular verbs to record in the vocabulary notebook that we suggested above. This will allow them to have this resource readily available when they are writing.

Spelling

Spell-check on the computer is a useful tool when your child is editing their work for proper spelling. They should go beyond this and read their paper aloud to ensure they are not missing any words that are spelled correctly but are not used in the proper way. An example would be the following: "Sam or I are best friends." The word *or* is spelled correctly, but *and* is the proper word to be used: "Sam *and* I." Spell-check will not catch this error. That is why taking the time to read their paper aloud is a good practice to impart.

You may also want to alert your child to words that sound alike but are spelled differently and mean different things—these are called "homophones," but there is no need to get that technical. Spell-check does not catch such errors either. These are words like *too*, *to*, and *two*, or *there*, *their*, and *they're*. Confusing these words in writing is a very common mistake—in fact, you may notice those errors made by adults when they post online.

Your child may have weekly spelling or vocabulary words to memorize. Ensure your child is learning these words and using them properly in their writing to help build their vocabulary and spelling knowledge.

Direct Quotes, Quotation Marks, and Dialogue

Proper use of quotation marks, quotations, and dialogue becomes increasingly important in middle school. The best way for your child to learn this skill is to read essays that use quote marks appropriately. You can employ the strategy we suggested in the "Research Writing" section, which is to read articles or essays, but in this case, read with the purpose of looking for quote marks placed around dialogue or passages of direct quotes others have written. After finding them, ask your child to rewrite them in their own words as a way to practice the skill.

The best place to see how to use quote marks properly within a sentence is to look at fiction stories at your child's grade level. Using dialogue correctly is a skill that develops with practice. Your child may be tasked with writing a story in their English class that includes dialogue. If they are given an assignment like this, look for samples that they can view so they can develop an idea of how to properly present dialogue in their writing.

Key Ideas about Dialogue and Quote Marks

The use of quotation marks differs depending on the position of dialogue in relation to the text around it. Commas and periods always go inside the quote marks. The first letter of spoken dialogue is capitalized. Here are examples:

BEGINNING	MIDDLE	BROKEN APART
"Caleb is a very smart person," said Vickie.	Vickie screamed, "I am so happy!" when she saw her grade on the report.	"If you finish early," the teacher said, "you can take a break."

The rules for question marks and exclamation points differ, depending on whether they are part of the quotation or not. For instance: *I wonder if she really told me to "Get lost!"*? This can be a complicated subject that your child may need to consult references to fully understand. Honestly, many adults have trouble with this topic.

Transitions

Transitions are used to help the reader easily transition between sentences without disrupting the flow of the writing. By middle school, your child should be familiar with using common transitional phrases to link sentences. Here are examples of common transitions used at the beginning, middle, and end of sentences in different types of writing.

TRANSITION WORDS

BEGINNING	MIDDLE	END
First	Next	Last
To Begin	Then	In conclusion
First off	Furthermore	Finally
Initially	Meanwhile	Eventually
Then	Now	At Last
One Morning	Suddenly	After all
To Start	After	In Summary
In the beginning	Gradually	Afterward
At the onset	Soon	Later on
Once upon a time	Later that day	In the end

By middle school, your child should have a repertoire of transition words that they use to make their writing flow.

Editing and Revision

Continue to support the editing and revision cycle by advising your child to use checklists like the one below, or those that your child's teacher provides for their writing assignments. Because your middle school child will need to write within different genres that have different requirements for formatting and content, ensure you ask the child's teacher for a guide that matches the writing assignment. In middle school, teachers often have specific things they are looking for in a writing assignment. These specifics are used to grade your child on their writing. Thus, understanding the expectation is very important.

Middle School Writing Checklist

- ❑ I have checked my grammar and spelling.
- ❑ I have checked to make sure my response answers the writing prompt of the assignment.
- ❑ I have ensured that my word choices are appropriate to the writing assignment.
- ❑ I have looked at the sentences I wrote to make sure I have included transitions where needed.
- ❑ I have reread my paper twice.

High School Writing

High school will require that students write across content areas and that they use their organizational skills to author pieces that are clear and concise. It is during high school that students learn to independently research topics and write on subjects to become mini experts by understanding what the expectations are so well they can explain it to someone else. This is how that expertise is exhibited. In this section, we share support for word choice, avoiding the use of slang and jargon, and ensuring that writing is clear and focused.

Word Choice

The choice of words becomes increasingly important as students are expected to write in more sophisticated styles. It is important to remind your child that using slang and jargon is not appropriate in professional writing. As a former high school writing teacher, I often had to remind students not to use slang, common acronyms, or abbreviations like LOL or OMG, and phrases that would be most appropriate when communicating with a friend. Emphasize the importance of using more formal language in writing, as casual word choice is a common error in high school composition.

Finding the right words to express an idea can be accomplished by using a thesaurus, which provides words with similar meanings that can be used to express ideas. Ensure that your child is reading the definition clearly so the synonym they choose retains the meaning they intended for the sentence.

Diversifying Sentence Types

Varying the types of sentences, including using compound and complex sentences, is a great way to make writing more interesting. High school students should begin to work on using varied sentence types to keep the reader engaged in their writing. Here are examples of three different sentence types that you can share with your child.

VARIED SENTENCE TYPES

SIMPLE SENTENCE	COMPOUND SENTENCE	COMPLEX SENTENCE
Orlando is a great city.	Orlando is a great city, and I enjoy spending summers there.	During my summer vacation in Orlando, I enjoyed going to amusements parks and museums, which made my trip memorable.

This chart shows examples of sentence types. The goal is to have your child go beyond merely using simple sentences in their writing; it is best to use a combination of sentence types. Encourage this practice by asking your child to identify the different sentence types they used when they are reviewing their writing.

Facts, Not Fiction

Fact-checking is important in high school writing and beyond. I taught English for many years, and one of the biggest errors I see in student writing is providing inaccurate facts. "Fact-checking" is a term we have repeatedly been hearing on the news in recent years. As a proficient writer, your child should make sure that any information they are including in their paper is backed up with evidence from the text or the research source they are using. Taking the time to ensure that their facts are accurate is an important step in the editing processes.

Focused and Clear Writing

Proficient writing is clear and concise. Your child should go over their writing to clean it up and make sure they are conveying their thoughts accurately, succinctly, and directly. Let them know they should not go on and on about a subject without making a specific point. In other words, they should avoid rambling. Remind your child that the purpose of writing is to convey messages that are clear and easy for the reader to interpret. Children should keep an eye out, too, for repetition. That is another very valuable use of the thesaurus—advise your child to look for words they often repeat, and then to come up with synonyms to vary the language and be as specific as possible.

What follows is a writing checklist for high school. Due to the varied writing types high school students encounter, the checklist can be used for both research and narrative writing.

High School Writing Checklist

- ❏ I have checked my grammar and spelling.
- ❏ I have checked to make sure my response answers the writing prompt of the assignment.
- ❏ I have included high-quality references.

❑ All of my references are also cited in the body of the paper.

❑ I have reread my paper twice.

Closing Thoughts on Writing

The complexity of the skill of writing expands as students move through the grade levels. As students progress in level, the expectations for their writing become increasingly more sophisticated. They are expected to expand on their writing by using more complex language, sentence structures, and coherence. The connection between reading and writing is very clear. Good writers are readers; thus, encouraging your child to read books in different genres will serve to enhance their writing skills. Providing your child with books that are at higher levels that offer diverse topics is optimal. Refer to our writing resources section in the Appendix for additional sources to consult about writing.

CHAPTER 10

HOW TO STAY UPBEAT AND NOT LOSE IT

You have done a lot of the work over the last few chapters. Your kids have a solid routine for learning, and you have established a set of parameters to ensure their attention is focused during their lessons. This is no small feat, and you should be very proud of yourself. You have survived the truly hardest parts of setting up an online learning environment and establishing the expectations of your child in the virtual learning environment. It takes teachers on average of three to four weeks to get all of this in place in the classroom. You are doing great, so take a few minutes to celebrate the work you have accomplished thus far.

From Surviving to Thriving: Your Self-Care Routine

We now want to get you out of survival mode and into a thriving situation as you support your child and keep your own self-care at the forefront. This chapter focuses on ensuring you take steps daily to refresh yourself as you maneuver through this truly difficult yet manageable world of online learning with your child. We'll offer some really helpful tips in this chapter that will be useful for years to come.

We have successfully put in place a morning routine for your child to ensure they start each day on track. As we noted, routines help us develop habits that are easy to follow. Once something becomes habit, you no longer dread it because it is part of your normal daily routine. Having a self-care regimen will help you maintain sanity during trying times. If you are running on empty, you will not be able to assist your child and may find yourself being irritable and lacking energy. Let's take a quick quiz to see where you fall in regard to self-care.

SELF-CARE QUIZ

On a scale of 1 to 10, with 1 the lowest and 10 the highest, how would you rate yourself on each of the following statements?

	Rating
1. I get seven to eight hours of sleep each night.	
2. I exercise three to five days per week.	
3. I set time aside each day for myself.	
4. I have a hobby that I enjoy and indulge in it at least twice a week.	
5. I feel energized most days.	
Total	

Results

SCORE 50–40: Excellent job! You are doing a great job with self-care—keep it up!

SCORE 39–30: Good job; you are doing some good things, but you need to ensure you are keeping a handle on self-care. Make a commitment to add at least one more day of relaxation to increase your harmony.

SCORE 29–0: There is more work to be done. You are doing some things for yourself, yes, but you need to add more self-care to your daily routine. Sit and write down three things that you will do differently starting tomorrow to build in more "you time."

So how did you do on your self-care quiz? If you scored high, congratulations on being in balance and taking time to refresh yourself so you can be the best you for your family!

If you scored in the middle range, again congratulations; you are getting there. With just a little help and focus, you will soon be thriving and feeling energized again.

If you scored at the lower end, do not fear; help is here. With a few adjustments in your thinking and in the way you prioritize your time, you will be thriving in no time. It just takes a commitment to establish self-care as an area of focus in your daily life. OK, let's get started on this most important journey.

What Is Self-Care?

You may be asking what self-care is and why a chapter like this is in a book about virtual learning. Self-care refers to the actions we take to ensure and preserve our health. This includes our physical and mental well-being. It is important because as an educator with more than two decades in the trenches, I can tell you that self-care saved me from burnout and despair. Teaching is one of the most demanding, noble, and yet thankless professions in the world. By now you can likely attest to this since you have been working at home with your child in a virtual setting. Teaching is one of the jobs with the highest burnout rates. Due to this, we spend a lot of time coaching teachers on how to take care of themselves so they are able to thrive in their career. I will share some tips in this chapter to get you thinking about self-care and hopefully provide you with a few strategies and ideas you can put into play to start on your self-care journey.

Facing Reality

Coming to grips with your self-care routine is the first step in the right direction. Do not deny it if you find that you are lacking in the self-care department. Again, this is normal for parents and caregivers. There is just so much time in the day. From getting the kids ready in the morning and caring for their needs throughout the day, it is easy to put your own needs on the back burner.

This is admirable, but not healthy. I am not scolding you here. I did this myself for years upon years. It wasn't until I realized one day that I was running on empty and was unable to give my family what they needed that I began to step back and take self-care more seriously.

During times of stress, we need to be filling our own bucket so that we are able to think clearly, make better decisions, and stay alert in the ever-changing world. This is really important if your kids are schooling at home with you. If you do not carve out time for yourself, you can find yourself without a spare moment to refresh.

Take another look at your self-care quiz and determine which area you want to focus on. Do you want to take up a hobby or ensure you exercise more? Set a specific goal so you can start your self-care journey.

Your Self-Care Tool Kit

There are only a few items that you will need in your self-care tool kit. These are items that I swear by when it comes to self-care. I have provided a list below. You probably have most of these items already in your home. Gather them and put them together in a space so that you can readily grab them when you need them. You can consider putting them together in a basket so you don't have to hunt for them when you want to use them.

Self-Care Tool Kit
- ❑ Journal
- ❑ Pen, pencil, or other writing utensil

❑ Candle to use for setting up a relaxing ambience. Sometimes just lighting a scented candle can do so much for relaxing you.

❑ Your favorite coffee cup or tea cup

❑ Your favorite type of coffee or tea

Success Tip: Assembling a success tool kit can be a game changer. Just engaging in a few things that you do frequently, which bring you pleasure, can make a huge difference in your level of joy.

Hobbies and Playtime

As adults, it is important that we continue to have hobbies and play dates for ourselves. To this day, I still love stickers and colored pencils, and I do paper art projects as a self-care activity. I also like to exercise as a way to stay healthy and relieve stress.

What are some hobbies and leisure activities that you can engage in? I want you to make a list of all the activities you enjoy doing for fun. It may take a minute for them to come to you if you have not engaged in them in some time, but don't give up. Keep thinking and they will come to you!

Activities/hobbies I enjoy:

_____

_____

_____

_____

_____

_____

Once you have the list, go through it and pick at least four activities that you will participate in. Make a commitment to do at least one of these activities each week at a minimum. If you can build in more time for them, that is great, but don't stress if you don't have the time to engage in the activity more than once a week. This will be an excellent start.

Tomorrow Is a New Day

Now, more than ever, you need to remember that if things don't go so well today, you always have tomorrow to start over and try again. As an educator, I had to consider that on many days. Maybe a lesson did not go the way I expected it. Maybe my routines were a disaster and I needed to scrap them and start over. Give yourself grace and understand that if things don't go well today, you have the gift of tomorrow to try again.

Being able to bounce back from mishaps is going to be very important when helping your child in the virtual learning space. You may have a day when your technology is down or your child may just be having an off time. The old adage, "This, too, shall pass," needs to be something you can tell yourself to get through those tough spots.

If you take on this attitude and realize that most days things won't go perfectly and that this is OK, as long as you have a plan to try to make things better tomorrow, then you are on the right track in regard to self-care.

Self-care is about facing reality and responding to it in ways that support your mental and physical health. Beating yourself up over a failed routine or a meltdown that you or your child have is not conducive to providing the positive reactions needed to continue on your road toward self-care. Taking care of yourself involves staying in tune with your emotions and responding immediately if you feel that you are heading down a negative pathway.

Check In with Yourself

A strategy you can use to keep a pulse on your mental and physical health is to quickly check in with yourself each day. Your check-in can be about one or two minutes—when you are alone somewhere, close your eyes and see how you are feeling.

Here are quick steps you can take for your one- to two-minute check-in. I would suggest doing this two or three times per day. It is intended to be a quick check, so make sure you are not going over three minutes. That is more than enough time to assess your feelings. Here are the steps I recommend.

Step 1: Get your journal and pen.

Step 2: Find a quiet area inside or outside the house where you won't be disturbed.

Step 3: Close your eyes and take three deep breaths.

Step 4: Ask yourself out loud: "How do I feel right now?"

Step 5: Answer yourself honestly. If you feel anxious, accept that.

Step 6: Think about why you responded the way you did. If you feel anxiety, what is causing that? If you feel happy, why are you happy right now? (Knowing these things will help you figure out what is triggering the feelings.)

Step 7: Own the feelings and tell yourself it is going to be OK.

Step 8: Write down how you are feeling in your journal, and when time permits, go back and consider the feeling and how you plan to combat it or continue it in the future.

Seeking Help

The tips I have shared have helped me get in tune with myself so I could maintain my self-care. If you find that you are really in a funk and cannot get out of it, please reach out for help. There are many organizations that provide assistance on how to manage stress. There is no shame in getting outside help. We want you to be healthy both physically and mentally so you can be your best you for your kids. In the Appendix on page 143, I have provided some agencies that you can look into for support.

Closing Thoughts on Self-Care

We have covered some really important practices in this chapter in regard to self-care. I think of all of the chapters in the book, this is a section you might want to think about revisiting as needed. We all fall into old habits, and if self-care is not something you have typically built into your routine, it can be easy to fall back into your old ways.

Remember to perform your self-checks a few times each day so you stay in tune with your feelings. Be sure to set up time weekly, if not daily, to do things you enjoy and that are healthy for you. Be OK with setbacks, and remember that tomorrow is a new day.

I hope that these tips are helpful for you as you continue to focus on being your best so you can be there for your kids. Remember, we are all in this together. In the next chapter, we will discuss ways to connect with your child's teacher, who you will find to be another source of help as you maneuver through virtual learning.

CHAPTER 11

FINAL THOUGHTS

"Trust yourself! You know more than you think you do!"

—Dr. Benjamin Spock

As we have explored the many facets of virtual learning, I hope that you have been able to take advantage of the tips and tools I have offered to help make the virtual learning experience more enjoyable for you and your child.

I want you to remember that you are not in this alone, and that reaching out to other parents is a good way to build a support network. We mentioned parent pods in Chapter One. I would recommend connecting with some parents and making time to talk, discussing the challenges and celebrations you are having with virtual learning. Virtual learning can already be an isolating experience; thus, if you can find ways to connect with others, it is a good way to keep from feeling all alone.

Family Time

Do not forgot to spend fun and recreational time with family and friends. Scheduling family time is essential to help make virtual learning a less overwhelming experience.

Plan it on weekends, after school, as time permits, and, of course, over summer vacations and school breaks. It's important to keep school time and family time separate.

Keep the Lines of Communication Open

Communicating with your child's teacher and school is pivotal. I want to again emphasize the importance of reaching out when you have questions. No question is a bad one and seeking clarification is important. I suggest reaching out every other week if possible just to check in and see if there is anything you can do to support your child at home. As we noted throughout the book, you do not want to wait until the last minute to begin to intervene. Early intervention is best, and this is only possible if you stay on top of your child's progress.

Don't Take Things Personally

Remember not to take things personally. Virtual learning can be very challenging. Things do not always go as we plan them, and we will make mistakes along the way. Keep an upbeat attitude and remember that flexibility is the key. Being flexible will allow you to sometimes just roll with the punches when the internet goes down, or a program does not work, or you experience any one of a plethora of other things that can go wrong. Give yourself a break and remember that you are doing your very best. This message should also be shared with your child. Students, too, can come down hard on themselves when they experience technical difficulties. Keep the mantra going that you are all doing your best and being flexible. This will help you overcome undue stress.

I wish you all the best as you work in the virtual learning world with your child. It is my hope that this book has been valuable to you, and you have been able to, and can continue to, implement the tips and techniques we've explored to make learning more manageable and fun!

APPENDIX

Here are some additional resources you may find helpful as you maneuver virtual learning.

Environment

Becker, Joshua. *Clutterfree with Kids: Change Your Thinking. Discover New Habits. Free Your Home.* Peoria, AZ: Becoming Minimalist, 2014.

Nelson, Mike. *Stop Clutter from Wrecking Your Family: Organize Your Children, Spouse, and Home.* Franklin Lakes, NJ: New Page Book, 2004.

Routines

Norman, Rachel, and Lauren Tamm. *Rhythms, Routines & Schedules: How to Simplify Life with Kids.* Scotts Valley, CA: CreateSpace, 2015.

Nadeau, Kathleen G. *Learning to Plan and Be Organized: Executive Function Skills for Kids with AD/HD.* Washington, DC: Magination Press, 2016.

Stein, Judith, Lynn Meltzer, Laura Pollica, and Kalyani Krishnan. *Parent Guide to Hassle-Free Homework: Proven Practices that Work from Experts in the Field.* New York: Scholastic Teaching Resources, 2007.

Setting Boundaries and Management

Costa, Jennifer. *The Conscious Parent's Guide to Positive Discipline: A Mindful Approach for Building A Healthy, Respectful Relationship with Your Child.* Avon, MA: Adams Media, 2016.

Hargis, Aubrey. *Toddler Discipline for Every Age and Stage: Effective Strategies to Tame Tantrums, Overcome Challenges, and Help Your Child Grow.* Emeryville, CA: Rockridge Press, 2018.

Self-Care

Hardy, Jayne. *Self-Care Project: How to Let Go of Frazzle and Make Time for You.* London: Orion Spring, 2017.

Pollak, Susan M. *Self-Compassion for Parents: Nurture Your Child by Caring for Yourself.* New York: Guilford Press, 2019.

Communication

Henderson, Anne T., Vivian R. Johnson, Karen L. Mapp, and Don Davies. *Beyond the Bake Sale: The Essential Guide to Family-School Partnerships.* New York: The New Press, 2007.

Lawrence-Lightfoot, Sara. *The Essential Conversation: What Parents and Teachers Can Learn From Each Other.* New York: Ballantine Books, 2004.

Technology

Calhoun, Joshua. *Reboot: If That Doesn't Work, Plug It In!.* Mustang, OK: Tate Publishing & Enterprises LLC, 2013.

Gookin, Dan. *Troubleshooting and Maintaining Your PC All-In-One for Dummies.* Hoboken, NJ: John Wiley & Sons, Inc., 2017.

Math

Benjamin, Arthur T., and Michael Shermer. *Teach Your Child Math: Making Math Fun for the Both of You*. Los Angeles: Lowell House, 1991.

Brennan, Jim. *The Everything Parent's Guide to Common Core Math: Grades K–5*. Avon, MA: Adams Media, 2015.

Sirois, Jamie L., and Adam A. Wiggin. *The Everything Parent's Guide to Common Core Math: Grades 6–8*. New York: Everything Publishing, 2015.

Reading

Durden, Felicia. *The Everything Parent's Guide to Common Core ELA: Grades K–5*. New York: Everything Publishing, 2015.

Mountain, Jill. *The Everything Parent's Guide to Common Core ELA: Grades 6–8*. New York: Everything Publishing, 2015.

Wise, Jessie, and Sara Buffington. *The Ordinary Parent's Guide to Teaching Reading*. Charles City, VA: The Well-Trained Mind Press, 2005.

Books for Read Alouds

Carle, Eric. *The Very Hungry Caterpillar*. Cleveland, OH: World Publishing Company, 1969.

Cowley, Joy, and Elizabeth Fuller. *Mrs. Wishy-Washy*. Auckland, New Zealand: Shortland Publications, 1985.

Davis, Viola, and Jody Wheeler. *Corduroy Takes a Bow*. New York: Viking Children's Books, 2018.

Henkes, Kevin. *Chrysanthemum*. New York: HarperCollins Publishers Inc., 1991.

Litwin, Eric, and James Dean. *Pete the Cat: Rocking in My School Shoes*. New York: HarperCollins Publishers, Inc., 2012.

Lobel, Arnold. *Frog and Toad Are Friends*. New York: HarperCollins Inc., 2003.

Martin Jr., Bill, and Eric Carle. *Brown Bear, Brown Bear, What Do You See?* NY: Henry Holt and Company, 1996.

Martin Jr., Bill, and John Archambault. *Chicka Chicka Boom Boom*. NY: Little Simon, 2012.

McCloskey, Robert. *Make Way for Ducklings*. New York: Viking Press, 1941.

Numeroff, Laura, and Felicia Bond. *If You Give a Mouse a Cookie*. New York: HarperCollins Inc., 1985.

Piper, Watty. *Little Engine That Could*. Racine, WI: Golden Press, 1976.

Rosen, Michael, and Helen Oxenbury. *We're Going on a Bear Hunt*. New York: Margaret K. McElderry Books, 2019.

Sendak, Maurice. *Where the Wild Things Are*. New York: HarperCollins Inc., 1963.

www.storylineonline.net
Storyline Online provides free videos of celebrities reading children books.

Writing

Day, Maisy. *101 Story Starters for Little Kids*. Self-published, 2020.

Dick, Lauren. *Early Start Academy, Learn Your Letters for Preschoolers*. Vancouver, BC: Engage Books, 2021.

Serravallo, Jennifer. *The Writing Strategies Book: Your Everything Guide to Developing Skilled Writers*. Portsmouth, NH: Heinemann, 2017.

Helpful Websites and Apps for Academics

Math Websites and Apps

Genius Kids (Apple)
This app allows kids to practice their multiplication facts. The games get increasingly more difficult as students increase their accuracy.

Kids Math (Android)

This app provides games that will help your child improve their math fluency. Kids can also practice addition and subtraction.

Khan Academy

www.khanacademy.org

Visit this website for free online courses for your child. Lessons provide step-by-step instructions on how to solve math concepts. (K–12)

Monster Math (Android)

Monster Math's games cover addition, subtraction, multiplication, division, and fractions. (K–5)

Moose Math (Android)

Moose Math takes kids on adventures where they practice counting, addition, subtraction, sorting, and geometry. Students can earn rewards to help build their own city and decorate buildings. (K–3)

SplashLearn (Android)

SplashLearn provides students with math games and practice they can use to improve their math skills. The colorful graphics and child-friendly activities are engaging for students. (K–5)

Starfall

www.starfall.com

Starfall's game-like math activities have colorful graphics that kids enjoy. (K–2)

Todo Math (Apple)

This app helps younger students learn basic math facts like addition, subtraction, and telling time by playing fun games.

Phonics Websites and Apps

Abcmouse.com

www.abcmouse.com

Abcmouse.com provides learning experiences for primary students. They offer a free 30-day trial. I would check them out to see if they can help your primary-grade student master their early literacy skills.

www.abcya.com

ABCya provides fun ABC games. (K–2)

Reading Websites and Apps

Funbrain Jr.
www.funbrainjr.com
Funbrain Jr. provides fun games and literacy activities, including worksheets.
(K–4)

Libby
www.overdrive.com
Libby allows middle school students to read library books on a tablet or
phone. (6–12)

Sightwords (Apple)
This app allows students to practice their sight words with flashwords and
games. (K–2)

www.skybrary.org
Skybrary offers hundreds of books that students can read or listen to. (K–5)

Starfall
www.starfall.com
Starfall provides reading games and lessons for students. (K–5)

Vocabulary Websites and Apps

Word of the Day (Android and Apple)
This app gives you a new word each day to learn. (5–12)

Daily Dictionary (Android)
This app notifies you of a new word each day. (5–12)

Writing Websites and Apps

Dexteria, Jr. (Apple)
Dexteria, Jr. is an app that helps young writers develop their fine motor skills.
(Pre-K)

Grammaropolis (Apple)
This app allows students to practice their grammar skills with engaging
characters. (K–8)

Journal Buddies
www.journalbuddies.com/prompts-by-grade/fun-writing-prompts-for
-middle-school
Journal Buddies provides writing prompts for students. (6–8)

Dotted Alphabet Paper

The following websites can be used to download letters of the alphabet with dotted lines for letter formation practice.

www.littledotseducation.com/free-alphabet-tracing-worksheets

www.printableparadise.com/printable-letter-tracing-worksheets.html

iTrace (Apple)
This app allows preschoolers to trace their letters. (Pre-K–1)

ACKNOWLEDGMENTS

This book is dedicated to all the parents, caretakers, and educators who sat in front of a computer with a child to help them learn virtually. Your impact will resonate for years to come.

Chuck, thank you for always being a number one cheerleader. I am blessed to have you in my life.

"Difficult roads often lead to beautiful destinations."—Unknown

ABOUT THE AUTHOR

Dr. Felicia Durden is an accomplished educator with over twenty years of experience. She has taught grades K–12 in her role as a reading specialist, served as an assistant director of reading and writing, and is a successful K–6 school principal in Phoenix, Arizona.

A Parent's Guide to Virtual Learning is Dr. Felicia's fourth book on education. She has a strong desire to provide families with tools to help their children have success in school. She believes that as your child's first teacher it is important that you are given tools and tips that will help you on your journey. Dr. Felicia enjoys reading and traveling with her family.